BENTLEY

CONTEMPORARY CUISINE

BENTLEY
CONTEMPORARY CUISINE

BRENT SAVAGE

WINE NICK HILDEBRANDT
PHOTOGRAPHY LUKE BURGESS

MURDOCH BOOKS

CONTENTS

MY COOKING   8

MASTERCLASS   14

APPETISERS   28

ENTRÉES   78

MAINS   128

DESSERTS   182

DRINKS   232

ACKNOWLEDGEMENTS   250

INDEX   252

MY COOKING

People often ask me "what is your style of cooking?". I find this difficult to answer. Rather than creating a style, cooking is about creating an experience. When people eat my food, I want it to be a simple pleasure. I want people to experience something unique, but the food should not be so complicated that it takes away from the occasion. When creating new dishes, there are many factors to consider — there are the obvious aspects such as seasonality, taste, texture and the balance of each dish but no matter what the cooking technique, the food should, above all, taste great. The food in this book is designed to be interesting but accessible. I hope to not only share the knowledge and expertise I have accumulated over the years working as a chef, but also my passion for food.

MAKING THE MOST OF THIS BOOK

In this book, I want to show you how to bring the food I make at Bentley into your kitchen. At the restaurant, I make all the recipes on a large scale, and use specialised equipment. It has been quite a challenge to think how the home cook could replicate these dishes.

I have written each recipe and broken it down into several sub-recipes so that each of these recipes can be used on its own or in conjunction with another recipe. I have scaled the proportions down as much as possible. However, some sub-recipes require a minimum amount to be successful, and will make more than you need for the final dish.

How you decide to use these recipes is up to you and I encourage you to not only try our combinations, but also to be creative. Use the recipes in your own way.

IN THE BEGINNING

When Nick Hildebrandt and I opened Bentley Restaurant & Bar in Sydney in March 2006, our mission was to change the way Australians approach food and wine.

In 2005, I was fortunate to be *The Sydney Morning Herald*'s Chef of the Year and, in that same year, Nick was named Sommelier of the Year. That was when our partnership was born.

Nick and I were two young guys with passion and experience, but without the budget to create the ideal restaurant. So we had to get creative. This has been indicative of our style and philosophy at Bentley. We wanted to create a restaurant that served great food and wine, but without the stiff and sterile environment that had dominated the dining scene.

FOOD

Like most chefs, I began cooking at a young age. Cooking was a way I could express myself but it also appealed to me because I knew it could take me to places I had never been before. The first real turning point came when I worked with chef Phillip Searle at Vulcans in Blackheath, New South Wales. Seeing the discipline and dedication it took to work in his kitchen made me see food and cooking in a new light. Cooking was no longer a task, it became a creation.

My first head chef position at Andrew McConnell's Mrs Jones in Melbourne really pushed me to be creative. The menu changed daily and the constant innovation this required helped define my personal style.

I believe quality produce is key in creating a wonderful dish. Wherever possible, I always use the best ingredients available, though I often find the most exciting dishes come about when we're trying to make the best we can with what we've got. The black sesame and pea fondant with goat's curd and snow peas (see page 98) is a good example of this. It is made primarily from sesame seeds, which most people would consider a garnish, not the basis of a dish. When working with different and out-of-the-ordinary ingredients such as these, I am challenged to find new ways of presenting them and am continually pushing the boundaries with different cooking techniques. To me, there is no such thing as 'experimental' or 'molecular' cuisine. Cooking is an ever-evolving scene, where every creation is a new experiment — whether using classic techniques or discovering new ways of cooking.

Technology is at the forefront of our field. Chefs have become accustomed to working with new equipment, ingredients and techniques. This evolution has given us a greater flexibility with what we can do with ingredients and produce. Where we used to require three to four pieces of equipment, we now use one piece to do all these processes simultaneously. The other advantage is that it also allows us to be more efficient and precise.

In 2005, I ate my way through Europe in search of inspiration for the menu at Bentley. I had some amazing meals at many Michelin-starred restaurants, but on that trip, my favourite thing to do was to spend nights dropping in at various bars, having a beer and a few bites to eat, then moving onto another, and continuing in this style until late in the evening — or the early hours of the morning — until I was full and satisfied. I loved the casual aspect of this Spanish way of dining. It was at once homely and contemporary. I wanted to capture that same energy at Bentley.

I take my main influences from Spain and France, but I also love spices, so Middle Eastern and Asian ingredients also appear throughout the menu. However, the produce is Australian, the menu is dictated by the Australian seasons and the flavours on the menu are as varied as our culture. Australia is a melting pot of food from all around the world, and to incorporate these contrasting worlds makes cooking a constant journey.

WINE

Wine plays a vital role in a meal whether at home or in a restaurant. In our opinion, every meal should begin with a glass of sparkling, a dry sherry or fresh riesling to prepare the palate. Nick has offered some food and wine pairings (see page 247) to illustrate the processes for choosing the best matches for the dishes in this book.

The wine list at Bentley is a constantly evolving document. Every wine on the list has a personality and tells a story. The goal is to give people something out of the ordinary, to introduce new wines to the public, wines which thrill and have a point of difference. Anybody with enough money can put together a list of big-name, trophy wines; anybody can buy Domaine de la Romanée-Conti, Lafite, Salon, Dom or Grange. These wines are not hard to get, but they don't necessarily make a great list. What makes a great list is a collection of hard-to-get yet interesting wines at prices to suit a variety of budgets.

Balance in a wine list is key. From vintage to styles to regions and producers, a well-balanced list will keep people interested. Having said that, some areas and varietals work beautifully with the food in this book, in particular Champagne, riesling and Burgundy.

EVOLUTION

Cooking is all about trial and error and trusting your own palate. I make these recipes every day and, still, I am constantly changing and pushing for better results.

The amazing thing about restaurants is that no matter how much you plan, organise and research, there are always unknowns and variables. The most astonishing thing is the way Bentley has taken on a personality and energy of its own. Sometimes the journey has been so exciting and intense that it seems the restaurant has been the one driving and Nick and I have merely been passengers on the ride.

Through these recipes, I hope to give you an insight into the restaurant, so that you can share my passion for food and wine at home with your friends and family.

BRENT

MASTERCLASS

During my career I have learned various cooking techniques, such as sous vide, hot smoking and dehydrating, which we apply to the recipes at Bentley. Some of these techniques require expensive equipment and elaborate set-ups. Most, however, can be slightly modified utilising domestic kitchen appliances. I will explain some of these techniques, so adventurous home cooks can achieve restaurant-quality results in their kitchen.

SOUS-VIDE COOKING

Sous vide is a modern cooking technique that involves cooking ingredients in vacuum-sealed bags. The bags are then placed in a water bath to cook, generally at low temperatures for an extended period of time. At the restaurant we find this technique to be extremely effective as it allows us to cook with precision and consistency, without compromising the best qualities in each ingredient.

EQUIPMENT

We use the following equipment for sous-vide cooking at Bentley. Although this may seem like an elaborate set-up and is expensive, you can replicate this cooking technique at home using everyday items. Indeed, when we first opened the restaurant we couldn't afford to buy the proper equipment, so we improvised as best we could.

Large saucepan
This is the vessel for your water bath.

Vacuum-seal machine and vacuum-seal bags
These ensure a watertight and airtight seal around the food, which create the necessary ennvironment and pressure for sous vide cooking.

To improvise at home, a zip-lock bag will mimic a vacuum-seal bag. To create a vacuum, simply place the desired food and any flavourings into a zip-lock bag. With the bag unzipped, lower it halfway into a large saucepan of heated water. This will expel the air out of the bag. Continue to lower the bag until you reach the zip, then zip the bag shut. This will ensure that there are no air pockets and will create a vacuum environment.

Thermoregulator
This device circulates the water in the water bath, ensuring a constant temperature throughout and no hot spots. This results in even cooking of the food.

To improvise at home, use a fish-tank pump placed in a large saucepan on the stove with a digital thermometer with a probe. The thermometer ensures an accurate measure of temperature (which is vital, otherwise your food will overcook or undercook) while the fish-tank pump circulates the water, maintaining a constant temperature.

COOKING TIMES

The sous-vide cooking technique is very versatile and can be used to cook a variety of ingredients, from meat and fish to fruit. To give you a general idea, below are some of the ingredients I like to sous vide with their cooking temperatures and times:

INGREDIENT	WEIGHT	TEMP	TIME
lamb rump	250 g (9 oz)	58°C (137°F)	3 hours
spatchcock ball	170 g (6 oz)	68°C (155°F)	20 minutes
pork neck	250 g (9 oz)	54°C (129°F)	3½ hours
duck breast	200 g (7 oz)	55°C (131°F)	35 minutes
chicken breast	200 g (7 oz)	63°C (145°F)	20 minutes
chicken leg meat	220 g (7¾ oz)	65°C (149°F)	1 hour

Remember that the temperature and time will vary depending on what you are cooking. Refer to each recipe for exact cooking temperatures and times.

HOT SMOKING

Hot smoking was a technique originally used to preserve food in the past. Today, it is widely used to enhance ingredients by imparting the delicate flavours of smoke. The results can vary depending on the type of wood chips used and the type of smoking technique applied. There are two main techniques: hot smoking and cold smoking.

At Bentley, we use a simple hot-smoking technique, as it has an effective and immediate result. Hot smoking is a very easy technique to use at home and clean, too, as it does not require charcoal. Hot smoking can be used with a variety of ingredients. Smoked fish, for example, although readily available, is a product we prefer to smoke ourselves at Bentley so we can control the quality, as well as achieve a specific desired flavour.

EQUIPMENT

Steaming apparatus
A large Chinese dumpling steamer or a saucepan with a steaming compartment is ideal.

Smoking chips
Wood chips for smoking are readily available from hardware stores and barbecue shops. We usually use hickory chips but you can also use maple, oak or apple wood.

METHOD

Place the smoking chips in the bottom half of a steamer and the ingredient to be smoked in the top half. Cover and place over high heat and once smoke appears, remove from the heat. Stand for about 8 minutes or until the smoke has evaporated. Remove the smoked item and use as directed in the recipe.

DEHYDRATING

Dehydrating is a technique we use a lot at Bentley. It is used to remove moisture from food, without cooking it, and intensifies flavours while adding a new dimension to the texture. This is not a new technique — it has been around for centuries as a means of preserving food, but many modern chefs use it in their cooking.

Dehydrated food can be stored for longer periods of time, which means this technique can be used to prepare food in advance. It is important when dehydrating food that the temperature is high enough so that bacteria does not form, but is low enough so as to not cook the food.

There are a few different ways to dehydrate food, including drying in the sun, in an oven, on the stove or using an electrical dehydrator. There are many affordable dehydrators available which makes this technique very easy to apply at home, however, the same results can be achieved using the simple appliances already available in your kitchen.

EQUIPMENT

Oven
To dehydrate food at home, use a conventional oven on the lowest temperature with the door slightly ajar to help with air-flow. Leave in the oven until completely dry. (You can use a fan-forced oven but you'll need to turn the fan-forced function off.)

Non-stick baking mats or baking trays
These are good for spreading out your ingredients, especially liquid mixtures.

DEHYDRATED CAPERS

100 g (3½ oz) salted capers, rinsed

Dry the capers with paper towel and place on a non-stick baking mat. Place on a baking tray and dry in a dehydrator at 60°C (315°F) for 4 hours. Alternatively, place in the oven on the lowest temperature and leave until completely dry. Remove and allow to cool. Store in an airtight container for up to 2 weeks.

BASICS

These recipes are the building blocks of our kitchen. These stocks and sauces will add depth of flavour to anything you cook. We make them fresh every day and suggest you make them as you need them so the flavour is not compromised.

WHITE CHICKEN STOCK

2 kg (4 lb 8 oz) chicken bones
2 stalks celery, chopped
1 carrot, chopped
1 onion, chopped
1 head garlic, halved widthways
2 fresh bay leaves
2 sprigs thyme

Chop the bones into medium pieces, place in a large saucepan, cover with water and bring to the boil. Drain, return the bones to the pan and cover with fresh cold water. Add the remaining ingredients, bring to the boil, then reduce the heat to low and simmer for 2½ hours, skimming the scum from the surface regularly. Strain, discarding the solids.

This can be made up to 1 day in advance and stored in an airtight container in the fridge. Makes 2 litres (70 fl oz).

CHICKEN JUS

6 spatchcock (baby chicken) bones and wings
60 ml (2 fl oz/¼ cup) vegetable oil
1 stalk celery, chopped
1 carrot, chopped
1 onion, chopped
1 head garlic, halved widthways
1 fresh bay leaf
4 sprigs thyme
1 litre (35 fl oz/4 cups) white chicken stock (see left)
20 ml (⅔ fl oz) lemon juice
sea salt flakes

Chop the bones and wings into small pieces. Heat the oil in a large saucepan over medium–high heat and cook the bones and wings until browned. Add the vegetables and garlic and cook for 2–3 minutes. Add the herbs, cover with the stock and bring to the boil, then reduce the heat to low and simmer for 1 hour, skimming the scum from the surface regularly. Strain, discarding the solids. Return the stock to a clean pan over medium heat and cook for 15 minutes or until reduced to a sauce consistency. Season with the lemon juice and salt.

This can be made up to 1 day in advance and stored in an airtight container in the fridge. Makes 300 ml (10½ fl oz).

LAMB STOCK

2 kg (4 lb 8 oz) lamb bones
400 ml (14 fl oz) white wine
2 teaspoons olive oil
2 stalks celery, chopped
1 carrot, chopped
1 onion, chopped
2 tomatoes, chopped
1 head garlic, halved widthways
2 fresh bay leaves
2 sprigs thyme

Preheat the oven to 180°C (350°F/Gas 4). Place the bones in a large flameproof roasting tray and roast for 40 minutes or until browned. Transfer the bones to a large saucepan and set aside.

Place the roasting tray over medium heat and deglaze with the wine, scraping the base to dislodge any cooked-on pieces. Cook until the wine is evaporated, then add the mixture to the bones.

Place the oil and remaining ingredients in a large frying pan over medium heat and cook until golden. Add to the bones.

Cover the bones and vegetables with water and bring to the boil, then reduce the heat to low and simmer for 2½ hours, skimming the scum from the surface regularly. Strain, discarding the solids. Return the stock to a clean pan, bring to a simmer and cook for 30 minutes or until reduced by three-quarters. Pass through a fine sieve, discarding the solids.

This can be made up to 2 days in advance and stored in an airtight container in the fridge. Makes 1 litre (35 fl oz/4 cups).

FISH STOCK

1 kg (2 lb 4 oz) fish bones
2 stalks celery, chopped
1 carrot, chopped
1 onion, chopped
1 head garlic, halved widthways
2 fresh bay leaves
2 sprigs thyme
10 black peppercorns

Chop the bones into medium pieces and rinse to remove any blood. Place in a large saucepan, cover with 1.5 litres (52 fl oz) water and bring to the boil. Add the remaining ingredients and bring back to the boil, then reduce the heat to low and simmer for 2½ hours, skimming the scum from the surface regularly. Strain, discarding the solids.

This can be made up to 1 day in advance and stored in an airtight container in the fridge. Makes 2 litres (70 fl oz).

VEAL JUS

2 kg (4 lb 8 oz) veal bones
400 ml (14 fl oz) red wine
2 teaspoons olive oil
2 stalks celery, chopped
1 carrot, chopped
1 onion, chopped
1 head garlic, halved widthways
2 fresh bay leaves
2 sprigs thyme

Preheat the oven to 180°C (350°F/Gas 4). Place the bones in a large flameproof roasting tray and roast for 40 minutes or until browned. Transfer the bones to a large saucepan and set aside.

Place the roasting tray over medium heat and deglaze with the wine, scraping the base to dislodge any cooked-on pieces. Cook until the wine is evaporated, then add the mixture to the bones.

Place the oil and remaining ingredients in a large frying pan over medium heat and cook until golden. Add to the bones.

Cover the bones and vegetables with water and bring to the boil, then reduce the heat to low and simmer for 2½ hours, skimming the scum from the surface regularly. Strain, discarding the solids. Return the stock to a clean pan, bring to a simmer and cook for 30 minutes or until reduced by half. Pass through a fine sieve, discarding the solids.

This can be made up to 2 days in advance and stored in an airtight container in the fridge. Makes 500 ml (35 fl oz/2 cups).

RED WINE JUS

2 stalks celery, chopped
1 carrot, chopped
1 onion, chopped
1 head garlic, halved widthways
2 fresh bay leaves
2 sprigs thyme
2 star anise
6 whole allspice
0.5 g fennel seeds
10 black peppercorns
20 ml (¾ fl oz) vegetable oil
750 ml (26 fl oz/3 cups) red wine
200 ml (7 fl oz) Port
500 ml (17 fl oz/2 cups) veal jus (see left)

Place the vegetables, garlic, herbs, spices and oil in a large saucepan over medium heat and cook until golden. Add the wine and Port and cook for about 20 minutes or until reduced to a glaze. Add the veal jus and bring to the boil, then reduce the heat to low–medium and simmer for 5 minutes. Strain, discarding the solids.

This can be made up to 2 days in advance and stored in an airtight container in the fridge. Makes 400 ml (14 fl oz).

AÏOLI

1 egg yolk
10 g (⅓ oz) Dijon mustard
2 teaspoons lemon juice
2 teaspoons white wine vinegar
1 garlic clove, crushed
sea salt flakes
200 ml (7 fl oz) olive oil
2 teaspoons Pernod Ricard or other pastis

Whisk together the egg yolk, mustard, lemon juice, vinegar, garlic and a pinch of salt in a bowl until thick and glossy. While whisking continuously, gradually drizzle in the oil, until thick and emulsified. Stir in the Pernod.

This can be made up to 3 days in advance and stored, covered closely with plastic wrap, in the fridge. Makes about 375 ml (13 fl oz/1½ cups).

CONFIT GARLIC

100 g (3½ oz) garlic cloves, peeled
150 ml (5 fl oz) vegetable oil

Place the garlic in a small saucepan and cover with the oil. Place over a very low heat and cook for 15–20 minutes or until very tender. Remove from the heat and allow to cool in the oil. Transfer the garlic and oil to an airtight container and refrigerate until required. Strain the garlic cloves before using — the oil can be reserved for cooking.
This can be made up to 3 days in advance.

ROASTED GARLIC PURÉE

4 heads garlic, halved widthways
50 ml (1½ fl oz) vegetable oil

Preheat the oven to 170°C (325°F/Gas 3). Place the garlic, cut-side down, in a roasting tray and drizzle over the oil. Roast for 15–20 minutes or until tender and golden — you may need to turn the garlic if it colours too quickly. Allow to cool, then peel. Place the cloves in an upright blender with the oil from the roasting tray and blend until smooth. Makes 200 ml (7 fl oz).
This can be made 3 days in advance and stored in an airtight container in the fridge.

CELERY SALT

2 stalks celery
50 g (1¾ oz) maltodextrin
5 g (⅙ oz) sea salt flakes

Thinly slice the celery and place in a bowl with the maltodextrin and salt and combine. Spread over a baking tray lined with baking paper. Dry in a dehydrator at 60°C (140°F) for 3 hours. Alternatively, place in the oven on the lowest temperature and leave until completely dry. Place the dehydrated celery in a spice grinder and grind into a fine powder.
This can be made 1 day in advance and stored in an airtight container in a dry place.

SUGAR SYRUP

100 g (3½ oz) caster (superfine) sugar

Place the sugar and 100 ml (3½ fl oz) water in a saucepan and bring to the boil. Stir until all the sugar is dissolved, then remove from the heat and allow to cool.
This can be made up to 1 week in advance and stored in an airtight container in the fridge. Makes 150 ml (5 fl oz).

GLOSSARY

INGREDIENT

AGAR AGAR A seaweed-based setting agent, this is used to thicken purées made from liquid. It sets at 35°C (95°F) and activates at 90°C (194°F). It's a great vegetarian substitute for gelatine. I prefer to use the powdered form. It's available from health food stores.

CALCIUM CHLORIDE A common salt used in cheesemaking. It is used with sodium alginate to form a gel seal and is available from gourmet food stores.

COUVERTURE This refers to a high-quality chocolate. The percentage of cocoa fat determines the richness, firmness and flavour. Choose a brand which is tempered.

EDIBLE FLOWERS Generally speaking, these are seasonal and include borage, rosemary, viola and fruit salad flowers. If one type is unavailable, substitute with another, bearing in mind each has its own unique flavour. Look out for them at farmer's markets and greengrocers.

FORUM CHARDONNAY VINEGAR A Spanish white wine vinegar available from gourmet food stores.

GELATINE Derived from collagen, gelatine is a tasteless and colourless setting agent. I use 5 g (⅛ oz) titanium-strength sheets, available from gourmet food stores.

GELLAN GUM A gelling agent with the ability to withstand high heat, it's ideal to use to make thermal reversible gels. It can also be used as a stabiliser and emulsifier. It's available in powdered form from gourmet food stores and specialty cooking stores.

GUAR GUM Derived from the guar bean, this is used as a thickening agent, emulsifier and stabiliser because it does not crystallise and prevents solid particles settling. It's available as a powder from health food stores.

IOTA A carrageenan extracted from red algae. It is used to produce soft gels and increase the viscosity of substances. It can also produce hot gels. It's available as a powder from gourmet food stores.

IRANIAN PISTACHIOS These extremely vibrant green nuts are of the highest quality. They're available from gourmet food stores.

ISOMALT Derived from beetroot, isomalt is an inverted sugar. It is sweet like sugar, but has the advantage of not crystallising as fast as granulated sugar. It's a white odourless powder, available from gourmet food stores.

KAPPA Like iota, this is a carrageenan extracted from red algae. It produces a gel with a firm, brittle texture. It's available as a powder from gourmet food stores.

KARA COCONUT CREAM I prefer to use this brand because it has a good consistency and excellent flavour. You can find it at Asian grocers.

LECITHIN Fatty substances found in animal and plant tissue. It is used as an emulsifier and is good for aerating sauces. It's available as a powder from health food stores.

LIQUID GLUCOSE This is derived from purified corn starch and is light yellow in colour. It is highly viscous and sweet. It's great to use because it does not crystallise and has a lower freezing point than granulated sugar. You can find it in the baking aisle of supermarkets.

LIQUID NITROGEN A clear, colourless liquid with a boiling point of -194°C (-317°F), used to freeze alcohols and quickly transform liquids into a hard brittle texture.

MALTODEXTRIN A carbohydrate made from modified corn or tapioca starch. Usually used as a bulking agent, it is also useful in absorbing excess oil without affecting flavours. It comes as a powder from gourmet food stores.

METHYLCELLULOSE This powder has the unique property of setting when hot and melting when cold (it needs to be chilled to 1–4°C/34–40°F to be activated). It's also used as an emulsifier. Buy it from gourmet food stores.

PECTIN Derived from fruits, including apples, pectin is a complex carbohydrate used as a thickening or gelling agent. It's available as a powder from health food stores.

SAMPHIRE Also known as sea asparagus, samphire is a type of edible plant which grows in coastal areas.

SODIUM ALGINATE Derived from seaweed, this is used in a technique called spherification, where it instantly forms a gel when it comes into contact with calcium. It's available as a powder from gourmet food stores.

SODIUM CITRATE This possesses a salty, mildly tart flavour. It's particularly good for neutralising acidity. It's available as a powder from gourmet food stores.

STABILISER (ICE CREAM) Ice-cream stabilisers are a mixture of gum, starches, emulsifiers and proteins. They suppress ice-crystal growth and improve the texture of ice creams and sorbets. It's available in powder form from gourmet food stores and specialty cooking suppliers.

TARTARIC ACID This has a sour flavour and is found naturally in plants, including grapes and bananas, and also wine. It's used to aid the gelling process, particularly when using pectin. It comes as a powder, which you can find in the baking aisle of supermarkets.

TONKA BEAN Originating from South America, it has an unique flavour. It was traditionally used in place of vanilla. Use in small amounts, as it's quite potent.

TRIMOLINE An inverted sugar, which means it is less susceptible to crystallisation, making it great to use in ice creams to create a smoother texture. It has a thick consistency and is available from specialist baking stores.

VEGETABLE CARBON Derived from burnt vegetable matter, this is used as a food colouring. It's available from specialist cake-decorating shops.

XANTHAN GUM Produced from the fermentation of glucose or sucrose, xanthan gum is used to increase the viscosity of a liquid. Unlike other stabilisers, it is very stable under a wide range of temperatures and also helps to stabilise emulsions by preventing oil separation. It's available as a powder from health food stores.

EQUIPMENT

ACETATE SHEETS We use these clear, flexible plastic sheets, available from art supply stores, in conjunction with moulds made from PVC piping to create smooth surfaces.

BOSTON SHAKER A cocktail-shaking apparatus consisting of a stainless steel body and a tall mixing glass called a boston glass. The glass is inverted onto the body and creates an airtight seal for shaking.

CREAM CANISTER Used to aerate liquids. It is 'charged' using nitrous oxide, which comes in small bulbs. Purchase a heat-sensitive version, which can handle both hot and cold liquids. Buy it from kitchenware stores.

DIGITAL SCALE This can measure in increments of 0.01 g and is necessary for recipes requiring small, precise amounts of ingredients. Buy it from tobacconists.

DOUBLE BOILER A stovetop apparatus consisting of a stainless steel saucepan placed over a pan of simmering water. This is used to gently melt chocolate or gelatine without burning or scorching them.

DRUM SIEVE (TAMIS) A sieve shaped like a snare drum used to achieve a fine, smooth texture. The food is pushed through using a scraper. You could also use a food mill (mouli or ricer) to achieve the same result.

MICROPLANE GRATER Used to finely grate food, including citrus zest, chocolate and nutmeg.

NON-STICK BAKING MAT This acts like baking paper and stops food from sticking. It's reusable and is very useful for dehydrating ingredients. The most common brand is Silpat, available from kitchenware stores.

PACOJET A Swiss food-processing system, which purées frozen substances into a creamy texture. It's perfect for making ice creams and sorbets.

PVC PIPING Available from hardware stores (they will cut it for you), it's great to use as a mould in conjunction with acetate to shape parfaits, ice creams and mousses.

THERMOMIX An advanced kitchen appliance with the ability to chop, beat, mix, whip, grind, knead, mince, grate, juice, blend, heat, stir, steam and weigh food.

THERMOMETER We most commonly use digital thermometers with a probe, as they give the most accurate reading and are useful with testing core temperature.

TECHNIQUE

CARTOUCHE A circle of baking paper which you put on top of a sauce or gravy to stop liquid from evaporating too quickly.

QUENELLE Traditionally, the word quenelle referred to a French dumpling filled with fish or meat. The term now more commonly refers to the technique used to create an oval shape from soft ingredients, shaped using 2 hot tablespoons or teaspoons.

APPETISERS

Dining out has evolved from the standard three-course meal. It is becoming more and more popular for people to share small plates of food and this style of dining is a relaxing way of entertaining at home. The following small plates range from the most simple things to prepare such as the marinated olives (see page 33) to some very intricate ones, the smoked eel parfait with white soy dressing and seaweed (see page 48), for example. Most of these appetisers can be prepared in advance, and also work well scaled down as canapés for a party.

GAZPACHO THREE WAYS

RED GAZPACHO

1 eschalot (French shallot), roughly chopped
1 long red chilli, roughly chopped
2 red tomatoes, roughly chopped
1 telegraph (long) cucumber, peeled
    and roughly chopped
1½ red capsicums (peppers), seeds removed
    and roughly chopped
5 confit garlic cloves (see page 25)
50 ml (1¾ fl oz) extra virgin olive oil
50 ml (1¾ fl oz) sherry vinegar
1 teaspoon Tabasco sauce
sea salt and freshly ground black pepper

Place all the ingredients and 100 ml (3½ fl oz water) in an upright blender (or food processor but the result will be less fine) and blend until very smooth. Season with salt and pepper, then refrigerate for 1 hour or until chilled and to allow the flavours to infuse. Pass through a fine sieve and serve.

This can be made up to 1 day in advance.

WHITE GAZPACHO

250 g (9 oz) crustless sourdough bread
300 g (10½ oz) blanched almonds
6 garlic cloves
300 ml (10½ fl oz) extra virgin olive oil
60 ml (2 fl oz/¼ cup) sherry vinegar
sea salt and freshly ground white pepper

Place the bread in a bowl, cover with water and soak for 10 minutes. Gently squeeze out the excess water using your hands and set aside.

Place the almonds, garlic, oil and vinegar in an upright blender and blend until smooth. Add the soaked bread and continue to blend until very smooth. Add water, if necessary, to make a pouring consistency. Season with salt and pepper, then refrigerate for 1 hour or until chilled and to allow the flavours to infuse. Pass through a fine sieve and serve.

This can be made up to 1 day in advance.

GREEN GAZPACHO

¼ bunch (20 g/¾ oz) basil, leaves picked
¼ bunch (20 g/¾ oz) dill, leaves picked
4 sprigs (20 g/¾ oz) flat-leaf (Italian) parsley,
    leaves picked
½ bunch (20 g/¾ oz) mint, leaves picked
50 ml (1¾ fl oz) extra virgin olive oil
2 eschalots (French shallots), roughly chopped
2 green tomatoes, roughly chopped
1 long green chilli, roughly chopped
1 telegraph (long) cucumber, peeled
    and roughly chopped
50 ml (1¾ fl oz) white wine vinegar
4 confit garlic cloves (see page 25)

Blanch all the herbs together in boiling water for 1 minute, then drain and refresh in iced water. Drain and transfer to an upright blender. Add the oil and blend until very smooth. Add the eschalot, tomato, chilli and cucumber, one by one, blending after each addition until smooth. Add 100 ml (3½ fl oz) water and the vinegar and blend until combined. Refrigerate for 1 hour or until chilled and to allow the flavours to infuse. Pass through a fine sieve and serve.

This should be made on the day of serving as it discolours on standing.

PRESENTATION

extra virgin olive oil, for drizzling
18 x 100 ml (3½ fl oz) glasses, for serving

Divide each gazpacho among 6 glasses. Finish each with a drizzle of oil. Place one of each type of gazpacho on a plate to serve. Serves 6 / each gazpacho makes 300 ml (10½ fl oz).

MARINATED OLIVES

70 g (2⅔ oz) Ligurian olives
70 g (2⅔ oz) Kalamata olives
70 g (2⅔ oz) Sicilian olives
1 sprig thyme
1 fresh bay leaf
1 star anise
1 cinnamon stick
2 g (¹⁄₁₆ oz) coriander seeds
5 black peppercorns
1 garlic clove
1 strip (4 x 2 cm/1½ x ¾ inch) of orange peel, white pith removed
1 strip (3 x 2 cm/1¼ x ¾ inch) of lemon peel, white pith removed
150 ml (5 fl oz) vegetable oil
100 ml (3½ fl oz) extra virgin olive oil

Place all the ingredients in a large saucepan and bring to the boil. Reduce the heat and simmer for 10 minutes. Remove from the heat and allow to cool. Spoon into a small bowl to serve.

To store, transfer the olives and oil to an airtight container and refrigerate for up to 4 weeks. Bring back to room temperature to serve. Fills a 500 ml (17 fl oz/2 cup) capacity jar.

BLUE SWIMMER CRAB AND MANGO WITH BLACK BEAN DRESSING

BLACK BEAN DRESSING

50 ml (1¾ fl oz) aged sherry vinegar
50 ml (1¾ fl oz) olive oil
1 long green chilli, seeds removed
1 garlic clove
1 eschalot (French shallot)
2 coriander (cilantro) roots
1 lime
25 g (1 oz) fermented black beans, soaked in water
    overnight and drained

Mix the vinegar and oil together in a small bowl. Finely chop the chilli, garlic, eschalot and coriander roots and add to the bowl. Using a microplane grater, grate half of the lime zest into the bowl, then juice the lime and add the juice to the bowl. Add the black beans and stir to combine. Set aside.

BLUE SWIMMER CRAB

250 g (9 oz) cooked blue swimmer crab meat
1 telegraph (long) cucumber, peeled, seeds removed
    and finely diced
4 sprigs (20 g/¾ oz) flat-leaf (Italian) parsley,
    leaves picked and chopped
¼ bunch (10 g/⅓ oz) mint, leaves picked and chopped
40 g (1½ oz) aïoli (see page 24)
3 teaspoons lemon juice, or to taste
sea salt and freshly ground black pepper

Combine all the ingredients in a bowl and season with lemon juice, salt and pepper. Set aside.

MANGO

1 green mango, peeled
1 quantity blue swimmer crab

Using a mandolin, thinly slice the mango lengthways into 1.5 mm (¹⁄₃₂ inch) thick slices. Lay 3 mango slices, just overlapping, on a work surface to form a rough 10 cm (4 inch) square. Repeat until you have 6 squares.

Place the crab mixture in the centre of each square, then roll up the mango to form cylinders. Trim the ends of the cylinders to neaten, then slice each widthways into 3 equal pieces. Set aside.

The rolls can be made up to 1 hour in advance and refrigerated.

PRESENTATION

chive shoots, for garnish

Place 3 pieces of mango and crab roll onto 6 plates. Lightly dress with the black bean dressing and top with the chive shoots. Serves 6.

CALAMARI WITH SQUID INK RICE AND GREEN CHILLI SALSA

GREEN CHILLI AND HERB SALSA

1 lime
3 garlic cloves, chopped
1 medium green chilli, coarsely chopped
35 ml (1⅕ fl oz) white wine vinegar
4 sprigs (20 g/¾ oz) flat-leaf (Italian) parsley,
    leaves picked
¼ bunch (10 g/⅓ oz) mint, leaves picked
2 sprigs (10 g/⅓ oz) dill, leaves picked
1 sprig (10 g/⅓ oz) basil, leaves picked
120 ml (4 fl oz) extra virgin olive oil
sea salt flakes

Using a microplane grater, finely grate one-half of the lime zest, then juice the lime. Place the lime zest, 2 teaspoons lime juice, the garlic, chilli and vinegar in an upright blender and blend into a fine paste. Add the herbs and oil and blend until smooth. Add a large pinch of salt and 2 teaspoons more of lime juice. Transfer to a chilled bowl, so the mixture cools quickly to preserve the bright green colour.

This can be made up to 12 hours in advance, covered closely with plastic wrap and refrigerated.

CALAMARI

250 g (9 oz) baby calamari
40 ml (1¼ fl oz) olive oil
2 teaspoons lemon juice
sea salt flakes

Clean the calamari leaving the skin intact. Separate the tubes from the tentacles. Heat the oil in a large frying pan over high heat, add the calamari tubes and cook for 1 minute, then add the tentacles and cook for another 20 seconds. Season with the lemon juice and salt. Serve immediately.

SQUID INK RICE

40 ml (1¼ fl oz) extra virgin olive oil
1 small onion, finely diced
1 garlic clove, sliced
200 g (7 oz/1 cup) medium-grain rice
2 fresh bay leaves
40 ml (1¼ fl oz) squid ink
450 ml (16 fl oz) fish stock (see page 23), hot
sea salt and freshly ground black pepper

Heat the oil in a heavy-based saucepan over medium heat. Add the onion and garlic and cook for 3 minutes or until softened. Add the rice and bay leaves, stirring to coat the grains well. Add the squid ink and cook for 1 minute.

Add half of the stock and bring to the boil. Gradually add the remaining stock, a little at a time, making sure it is absorbed before adding more. Stir occasionally and cook until the rice is al dente. Season with salt and pepper. Serve immediately.

PRESENTATION

Dab the salsa onto 6 plates. Using 2 tablespoons, place 2 quenelles of squid ink rice onto each plate. Scatter over the calamari. Serves 6.

PICKLED BONITO WITH PRESERVED LEMON AND APPLE

CURED BONITO

100 g (3½ oz/¾ cup) sea salt flakes
100 g (3½ oz) caster (superfine) sugar
180 g (6½ oz) piece of bonito fillet, skin on

Mix the salt and sugar together. Remove any bones from the bonito, then halve lengthways. Sprinkle the salt and sugar mixture evenly over the bonito flesh and refrigerate for 1 hour, then rinse off the salt and sugar and pat dry.

PICKLED BONITO

125 g (4½ oz) caster (superfine) sugar
5 whole allspice
1 fresh bay leaf
200 ml (7 fl oz) red wine vinegar
1 quantity cured bonito

Place the sugar, allspice, bay leaf, vinegar and 150 ml (5 fl oz) water in a small saucepan and bring to the boil, stirring until the sugar is dissolved. Remove from the heat and cool to room temperature, then refrigerate until chilled. Add the cured bonito and leave to pickle in the fridge for 3 hours.

Drain well, discarding the pickling liquid. Remove the skin from the bonito and discard. Slice the bonito into 5 mm (¼ inch) thick pieces and serve immediately.

If not serving immediately, wrap the pickled bonito in paper towel, then plastic wrap and refrigerate for up to 2 days.

PRESERVED LEMON PURÉE

2 store-bought preserved lemons
100 ml (3½ fl oz) olive oil

Rinse the lemons. Remove the pulp and place in a small saucepan. Use a knife to cut the white pith from the peel and discard the peel (or reserve for another use). Add the pith to the pulp. Add 200 ml (7 fl oz) water and bring to the boil for 1 minute, then drain and refresh in cold water. Blanch, refresh and drain again, then transfer to an upright blender. Add the oil and blend until very smooth. Set aside.

APPLE SALAD

½ green apple, peeled and core removed
1 eschalot (French shallot)
½ bunch (10 g/⅓ oz) chives
2 teaspoons olive oil
1 teaspoon lemon juice
20 g (¾ oz) Avruga (see note)
sea salt and freshly ground black pepper

Finely dice the apple and eschalot. Finely chop the chives. Combine these with the oil and lemon juice. Gently stir in the Avruga and season with salt and pepper. Serve immediately.

NOTE Avruga is herring roe, available from select fishmongers.

PRESENTATION

Place a slice of bonito onto 6 spoons, top with a little apple salad and place a dollop of the lemon purée alongside. Serves 6.

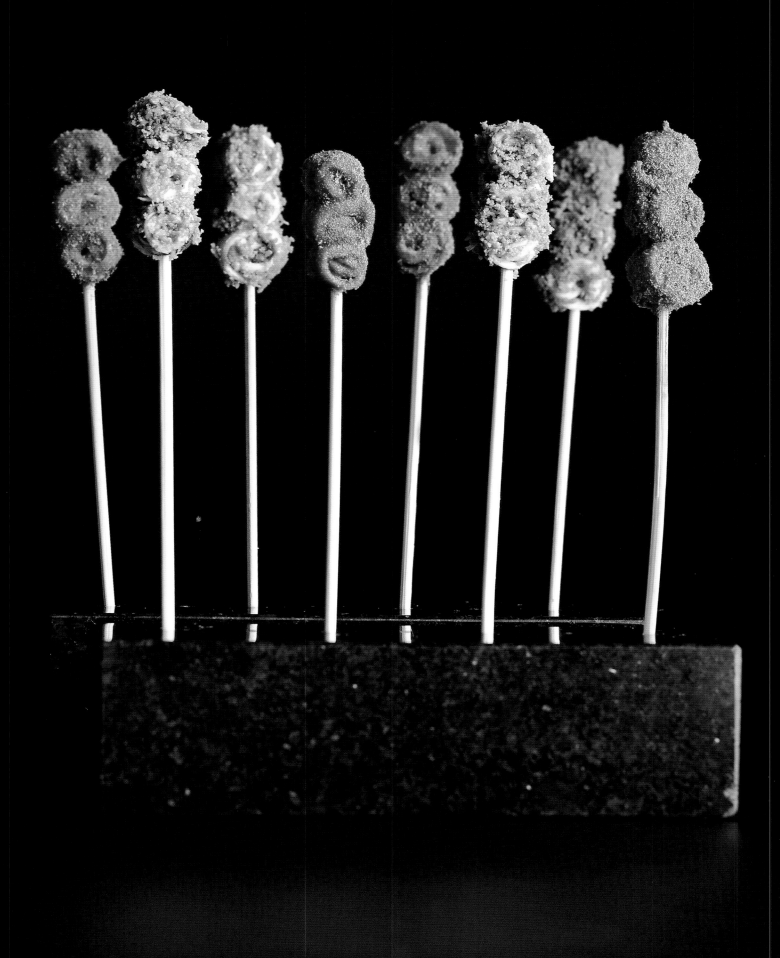

WHITE ANCHOVY STICKS

WHITE ANCHOVY STICKS WITH PISTACHIO PRALINE

50 g (1¾ oz) caster (superfine) sugar
100 g (3½ oz/¾ cup) Iranian pistachio kernels
40 g (1½ oz/⅔ cup) panko breadcrumbs (see Note)
5 g (⅙ oz) sea salt flakes
12 marinated white anchovy fillets
4 bamboo skewers

Combine the sugar and 30 ml (1 fl oz) water in a small saucepan over medium–high heat and cook, without stirring, until it reaches 118°C (245°F) and forms a caramel. Remove from the heat, and stir in the pistachios. Spread onto a 30 x 20 cm (12 x 8 inch) tray lined with baking paper and allow to cool.

Break the praline into pieces and finely crush using a mortar and pestle. Stir in the breadcrumbs and salt.

This can be made up to 2 days in advance and stored in an airtight container in the fridge. When ready to serve, roll each anchovy tightly, then skewer 3 rounds onto each skewer. Roll in enough praline mixture to lightly coat. Serves 4.

NOTE Panko breadcrumbs are Japanese breadcrumbs with a coarse texture. They are available from Asian grocers. You can substitute fresh breadcrumbs.

WHITE ANCHOVY STICKS WITH TOMATO AND PAPRIKA

45 g (1¾ oz) freeze-dried tomato powder (see Note)
5 g (⅙ oz) smoked paprika
30 g (1 oz/½ cup) panko breadcrumbs (see Note above)
5 g (⅙ oz) sea salt flakes
12 marinated white anchovy fillets
4 bamboo skewers

Place the tomato powder, paprika, breadcrumbs and salt in a bowl and combine.

Roll each anchovy tightly, then skewer 3 rounds onto each skewer. Roll in enough tomato powder to lightly coat. Serve immediately. Serves 4.

NOTE Freeze-dried tomato powder is dehydrated tomato. It is available from select health food stores and gourmet food stores.

TUNA TARTARE WITH TOMATO AND SQUID INK

TOMATO DRESSING

4 vine-ripened tomatoes
1 eschalot (French shallot)
1 garlic clove
30 ml (1 fl oz) extra virgin olive oil
sea salt and freshly ground black pepper

Place the tomato, eschalot, garlic and oil in an upright blender and blend until smooth. Season with salt and pepper. Pass through a fine sieve, discarding the pulp.

This can be made 1 day in advance and stored in an airtight container in the fridge.

SQUID INK DRESSING

150 ml (5 fl oz) tomato dressing
20 ml (¾ fl oz) squid ink

Place the tomato dressing in a small saucepan over medium heat and bring to the boil. Continue to cook until the liquid is reduced to 100 ml (3½ fl oz). Stir through the squid ink. Allow to cool, then transfer to a sauce bottle.

This can be made 1 day in advance and stored in an airtight container in the fridge.

CROÛTONS

150 g (5½ oz) sourdough bread, crusts removed
30 ml (1 fl oz) olive oil

Preheat the oven to 170°C (325°F/Gas 3). Dice the bread into 1 cm (½ inch) cubes and coat with the oil. Bake for 8 minutes or until crisp and golden. Set aside to cool.

TUNA TARTARE

350 g (12 oz) piece of yellowfin tuna
3 teaspoons extra virgin olive oil
sea salt and freshly ground white pepper

Dice the tuna into 1 cm (½ inch) cubes. Combine with the oil and season with salt and pepper.

This can be made 1 hour in advance and stored in an airtight container in the fridge.

AVOCADO PURÉE

1 ripe avocado
1 teaspoon lemon juice
2 teaspoons extra virgin olive oil
sea salt and freshly ground black pepper

Peel the avocado and remove the stone. Pass the flesh through a fine sieve. Stir in the lemon juice and oil and season with salt and pepper. Set aside.

PRESENTATION

Arrange the tuna in 6 bowls. Using 2 teaspoons, place a quenelle of avocado purée to one side of each bowl. Dot the squid ink dressing around alternating with the croûtons. Finish with a drizzle of tomato dressing. Serves 6.

COD AND POTATO CROSTINI

COD

200 g (7 oz) piece of cod fillet (such as blue-eye
    trevalla or hapuka), skin removed
60 g (2¼ oz) sea salt flakes
200 ml (7 fl oz) milk
1 fresh bay leaf
2 sprigs thyme
6 black peppercorns

Trim any bloodline from the cod. Place on a plate, sprinkle both sides with the salt, cover with plastic wrap and refrigerate for 1½ hours to draw out the moisture.

Rinse the salt from the cod. Place the milk, bay leaf, thyme and peppercorns in a saucepan over low heat and simmer for 15 minutes to allow the flavours to infuse. Add the cod and cook for 8 minutes or until cooked through. Allow to cool in the milk. Remove the cod and set aside. Strain the milk and reserve.

POTATO

50 ml (1¾ fl oz) extra virgin olive oil
50 g (1¾ oz) brown onion, diced
200 g (7 oz) desiree potato, diced
1 quantity cod
40 ml (1¼ fl oz) infused milk (reserved from cod)
sea salt and freshly ground black pepper

Heat the oil in a small saucepan over medium heat. Add the onion and cook for 1 minute. Add the potato and enough water to cover, then reduce the heat to low and cook for 15 minutes or until the potato is tender. Strain, then transfer the potato to a food processor.

Add the cod and the reserved cod milk and process until smooth. Season with salt and pepper.

MUSTARD CREAM

50 ml (1¾ fl oz) pouring (single) cream
1 tablespoon Dijon mustard
sea salt flakes

Whisk the cream, mustard and a pinch of salt together until very soft peaks form. Place in a piping bag fitted with a 5 mm (¼ inch) plain nozzle. Refrigerate until ready to serve.

CROSTINI

½ baguette
30 ml (1 fl oz) olive oil
sea salt flakes

Preheat the oven to 160°C (315°F/Gas 2–3). Slice the baguette into thirty-six 2 mm (¹⁄₁₆ inch) thick slices and arrange in a single layer on baking trays. Drizzle with the oil and sprinkle with salt. Bake for 5 minutes or until crisp. Remove from the oven and cool.

PRESENTATION

½ bunch (10 g/⅓ oz) chives, finely chopped
finely grated zest of 1 lemon

Spoon 70 g (2½ oz) of the cod and potato mixture onto each plate. Pipe the mustard cream over the top, sprinkle with the chives and lemon zest, then insert 6 crostini into each cod and potato mixture. Serves 6.

This is one of my favourite recipes. I love the flavour of smoked eel, but I find the textures to be inconsistent — often the outer edges are dry and stringy and the centre soft and mushy. The creaminess of parfait seems to be the perfect solution. This dish allows me to enjoy the best of both worlds.

SMOKED EEL PARFAIT WITH WHITE SOY DRESSING AND SEAWEED

KOMBU CHIPS

125 g (4½ oz) sebago potato, roughly chopped
10 g (⅓ oz) dried kombu (see Note)
vegetable oil, for deep-frying

Place the potato in a saucepan of cold water, bring to the boil and cook until falling apart. Drain, then transfer to an upright blender. Add 200 ml (7 fl oz) fresh boiled water and blend until a batter consistency. Cool, then refrigerate for at least 1 day to allow the air to expel from the mixture.

Spread the mixture evenly onto a non-stick baking mat to 2 mm (¹⁄₁₆ inch) thick. Finely chop the kombu and sprinkle over the mixture.

Place on a baking tray and dry in a dehydrator at 60°C (140°F) for 2 hours. Alternatively, place in the oven on the lowest temperature and leave until completely dry.

When ready to serve, heat the oil to 175°C (347°F). Break the dehydrated potato and kombu into 5 cm (2 inch) squares and deep-fry for 2 seconds. Turn out onto a board, cover with a clean tea towel (dish towel) and use your hands to flatten completely. Trim into 2 cm (¾ inch) squares.

NOTE Dried kombu is a type of kelp, available from Asian grocers.

SMOKED EEL PARFAIT

1 length 1.5 cm (⅝ inch) diameter PVC piping
1 sheet acetate
2 sheets gelatine, titanium strength
400 ml (14 fl oz) milk
50 ml (1¾ fl oz) pouring (single) cream
1 garlic clove
1 g (¹⁄₃₂ oz) kappa
30 g (1 oz) unsalted butter
80 g (2¾ oz) smoked eel, skin and bones removed

Cut the PVC piping into six 10 cm (4 inch) long pieces. Cut the acetate into six 12 x 5 cm (4½ x 2 inch) rectangles. Roll each piece widthways, then place each roll inside a piece of PVC pipe. Make sure one end of the acetate sits flush with the pipe and the other end protrudes. Place plastic wrap over the flush end and secure with tape. Stand, covered-end down, on a tray.

Soak the gelatine in cold water for 5 minutes or until softened. Place the milk, cream, garlic, kappa and butter in a saucepan and, using a stick blender, blend until combined. Bring to the boil. Squeeze out the excess water from the gelatine, then add the gelatine to the pan, stirring to dissolve. Remove from the heat.

Place the smoked eel in a food processor and process until smooth. With the motor running, gradually add the hot milk mixture and process until well combined and smooth. Pour into the moulds, filling only to the top of the pipe, then refrigerate for 2–3 hours or until set.

These can be made up to 1 day in advance and stored in the fridge in an airtight container. This recipe makes more than you will need.

CELERY JELLY

600 g (1 lb 5 oz) celery
20 g (¾ oz) English spinach leaves
2 sheets gelatine, titanium strength
3 g (⅒ oz) iota

Remove the celery leaves and reserve. Trim the base of the celery and discard. Cut the celery into 5 mm (¼ inch) pieces and place in a saucepan. Cover with water and simmer for 10 minutes or until tender. Allow the celery to cool in the liquid.

Meanwhile, blanch the celery and spinach leaves in boiling water for 1 minute. Drain and refresh in iced water. Drain again and transfer to an upright blender.

Add the cooled celery and cooking liquid to the blender and blend until smooth. Pass through a fine sieve, discarding the solids.

Soak the gelatine in cold water for 5 minutes or until softened.

Measure out 300 ml (10½ fl oz) of the celery and spinach purée into a clean saucepan. Add the iota and heat to 85°C (185°F). Remove from the heat. Squeeze out the excess water from the gelatine, add the gelatine to the pan and whisk until dissolved. Pour the mixture into a shallow 40 x 30 cm (16 x 12 inch) tray lined with freezer film and refrigerate for 1 hour or until set.

This should be made on the day of serving.

WHITE SOY DRESSING

50 ml (1¾ fl oz) white soy sauce
30 ml (1 fl oz) rice wine vinegar
30 ml (1 fl oz) mirin
2 drops sesame oil
60 g (2¼ oz/¼ cup) sour cream
0.5 g xanthan gum

Mix the soy sauce, vinegar, mirin and sesame oil together in a stainless steel bowl. Add the sour cream and xanthan gum and stir until combined.

This can be made 1 day in advance and stored in an airtight container in the fridge.

SEAWEED AND MUSTARD CRESS SALAD

80 g (2¾ oz) white tosaka (see Note)
80 g (2¾ oz) red tosaka (see Note)
80 g (2¾ oz) green tosaka (see Note)
40 g (1½ oz) mustard cress
2 teaspoons extra virgin olive oil
1 teaspoon lemon juice

Wash the salt from the tosaka and tear into small pieces. Combine with the cress in a small bowl and dress with the oil and lemon juice. Serve immediately.

NOTE Tosaka is a type of salted seaweed. It is available frozen from Japanese grocers.

PRESENTATION

5 g (⅙ oz) dried kombu (see Note, opposite), finely chopped
celery salt (see page 25), for garnish

Remove the jelly and parfaits from the fridge. Slide the jelly and freezer film off the tray and onto a work surface. To remove the parfaits, remove the plastic wrap and tape, then use the protruding acetate to carefully pull them out of the moulds — the acetate will naturally uncurl from around the parfaits. Use the acetate to transfer the parfaits onto the jelly, placing the first one about 1 cm (½ inch) from the short edge, then spacing the others evenly apart. Using a sharp knife, cut the jelly and the freezer film between the parfaits, so that each jelly strip is about 5 cm (2 inches) wide. Working with one at a time and using the freezer film as a guide, carefully roll the jelly strip around the parfait to enclose it completely. Trim the excess jelly from the ends of each parfait. Cut each parfait into 2 pieces.

Place the parfaits onto plates, arrange the dried kombu and celery salt in a line alongside. Dress the plate with some white soy dressing. Place some seaweed salad on the plate and insert the kombu chips into the salad. Serves 6.

PRAWN ON A STICK WITH
BLACK AND WHITE SESAME

PRAWN STICKS

6 raw (green) banana prawns (shrimp)
6 short bamboo skewers
20 ml (⅔ fl oz) vegetable oil

Peel the prawns and remove the heads and tails. Thread a prawn onto each skewer. Heat the oil in a frying pan over high heat. Add the prawns and cook for 1 minute each side or until just cooked through. Serve immediately.

PRESENTATION

30 g (1 oz) white sesame seeds, toasted
30 g (1 oz) black sesame seeds, toasted
30 g (1 oz) aïoli (see page 24)

Coat the prawns in the sesame seeds and serve with the aïoli for dipping. Serves 6.

PARMESAN CUSTARD WITH TRUFFLED ASPARAGUS

SEMOLINA CRACKERS

75 ml (2⅔ fl oz) milk
12 g (⅖ oz) unsalted butter
125 g (4½ oz) plain (all-purpose) flour,
    plus extra for dusting
35 g (1¼ oz) fine semolina
1 g (1/32 oz) sea salt flakes
½ teaspoon baking powder

Heat the milk and butter in a small saucepan to 60°C (140°F).

Place the remaining ingredients in the bowl of an electric mixer fitted with a dough hook. With the mixer on low speed, gradually pour in the warm milk mixture and mix until the dough comes together and is smooth. Wrap in plastic wrap and rest for 20 minutes at room temperature.

Preheat the oven to 170°C (325°F/Gas 3).

Lightly dust the rollers of a pasta machine. Roll the dough out through each setting on the pasta machine, beginning at the largest setting until about 1 mm (1/32 inch) thick. Cut into 3 cm (1¼ inch) squares, place on a baking tray lined with baking paper and bake for 10 minutes or until puffed and lightly golden. Allow to cool on the trays.

These will keep in an airtight container for up to 2 days.

PARMESAN CUSTARD

150 g (5½ oz/1½ cups) finely grated Parmigiano-
    Reggiano parmesan
100 ml (3½ fl oz) milk
4 eggs, lightly beaten

Combine the parmesan, milk and 100 ml (3½ fl oz) water in a saucepan over low–medium heat, stirring until the parmesan is melted. Reduce the heat to low and whisk in the beaten egg. Cook, stirring, until the mixture thickens and reaches 85°C (185°F), about 10 minutes. The mixture will separate and appear curdled. Cool to room temperature, then refrigerate for 1 hour or until chilled.

Place the mixture in an upright blender or food processor and blend until smooth. Transfer to a piping bag fitted with a 1.5 cm (⅝ inch) plain nozzle and refrigerate to firm up slightly before serving.

TRUFFLED ASPARAGUS

200 g (7 oz) asparagus, trimmed
20 ml (⅔ fl oz) truffle oil (see Note)
1 garlic clove
50 g (1¾ oz) fresh black truffles, thinly sliced

Thinly slice the asparagus stalks into rounds, leaving the tips whole. Blend the truffle oil and garlic in an upright blender to form a coarse paste. Marinate the asparagus and sliced truffle in the truffle mixture for 1 hour in the fridge.

NOTE Truffle oil is available from gourmet food stores.

PRESENTATION

Pipe the parmesan custard onto plates. Spoon the truffled asparagus alongside and scatter around the crackers. Serves 6.

KINGFISH CEVICHE WITH PICKLED DAIKON AND YUZU MAYONNAISE

PICKLED DAIKON

300 g (10½ oz) daikon (about ½ small)
35 ml (1⅕ fl oz) yuzu juice (see Note)
3 teaspoons dai dai (see Note)
5 g (⅙ oz) caster (superfine) sugar
sea salt flakes

Peel the daikon. Using a mandolin, slice it lengthways into 1 mm (¹⁄₃₂ inch) thick slices. Stack 3–4 slices on top of each other, roll up tightly, then cut widthways into 3 mm (⅛ inch) thick strips to form 'noodles'.

Whisk together the yuzu juice, dai dai, sugar and 25 ml (⅘ fl oz) water in a bowl until well combined and the sugar is dissolved. Season to taste with salt.

Add the daikon to the bowl and toss to coat. Place in a large zip-lock bag and refrigerate for at least 1 hour. Drain well before serving.

This can be made up to 12 hours in advance.

NOTE Dai dai is a type of ponzu sauce and yuzu is a Japanese citrus. Both are available from Japanese grocers.

YUZU MAYONNAISE

1 egg
1 egg yolk
25 ml (⅘ fl oz) yuzu juice (see Note above)
2 teaspoons dai dai (see Note above)
350 ml (12 fl oz) vegetable oil

Whisk together the egg, egg yolk, yuzu juice and dai dai in a bowl until combined. While whisking, gradually pour in the oil, whisking until thick and emulsified. Transfer to a piping bag fitted with a 2 mm (¹⁄₁₆ inch) plain nozzle and refrigerate until ready to serve.

This will keep for up to 1 week covered closely with plastic wrap in the fridge.

KINGFISH

300 g (10½ oz) piece of kingfish belly, skin off

Trim the kingfish and slice lengthways into 2 mm (¹⁄₁₆ inch) thick slices, then trim to 6 cm (2½ inch) long pieces. Cut the slices lengthways into 2 mm (¹⁄₁₆ inch) thick noodle-like strips. Serve immediately.

PRESENTATION

60 ml (2 fl oz/¼ cup) olive oil
½ bunch (10 g/⅓ oz) chives, finely chopped
½ bunch (30 g/1 oz) coriander (cilantro), stems finely
    chopped and small leaves reserved for garnish
sea salt and freshly ground black pepper
10 g (⅓ oz) togarashi pepper (see Note)

Combine the kingfish and pickled daikon. Add the oil, chives and coriander stem, season with salt and pepper and combine. Place onto 6 plates and garnish with the coriander leaves. Pipe small dollops of yuzu mayonnaise around the kingfish and sprinkle the togarashi pepper over the mayonnaise. Serves 6.

NOTE Togarashi pepper is ground Japanese chilli pepper available from Asian grocers.

CROÛTONS

150 g (5½ oz) sourdough bread, crusts removed
30 ml (1 fl oz) olive oil

Preheat the oven to 170°C (325°F/Gas 3). Dice the bread into 1 cm (½ inch) cubes and coat with the oil. Bake for 8 minutes or until crisp and golden. Set aside to cool.

SHERRY VINAIGRETTE

75 ml (2⅔ fl oz) olive oil
25 ml (⅘ fl oz) sherry vinegar
25 ml (⅘ fl oz) vegetable oil
5 g (⅙ oz) sea salt flakes

Whisk all the ingredients together until the salt is dissolved. Set aside.

VENISON TARTARE

400 g (14 oz) piece of venison fillet, trimmed
½ telegraph (long) cucumber, peeled and seeds removed
40 g (1½ oz) salted baby capers, soaked in water
    for 20 minutes, then drained
1 bunch (20 g/⅔ oz) chives, finely chopped
1 eschalot (French shallot), finely diced
½ quantity sherry vinaigrette, or to taste
sea salt and freshly ground black pepper

Dice the venison into 1 cm (½ inch) cubes. Dice the cucumber into 5 mm (¼ inch) cubes. Combine both with the capers, chives, eschalot and the vinaigrette in a bowl and toss to coat. Add a little more vinaigrette, if desired. Season with salt and pepper. Serve immediately.

SWEET LIQUID WASABI

6 g (⅕ oz) calcium chloride
200 g (7 oz) honey
40 g (1½ oz) wasabi paste
2.5 g (1⁄12 oz) sodium alginate
1 g (1⁄32 oz) sodium citrate
juice of 1 lime
a pinch of sea salt flakes

Combine the calcium chloride with 500 ml (17 fl oz/2 cups) cold water. Set the calcium bath aside.

Combine the remaining ingredients and 200 ml (7 fl oz) water in an upright blender and blend until smooth, then transfer to a bowl. Using a teaspoon, drop the wasabi mixture into the calcium bath, placing in no more than 10 drops at a time. Leave in the bath for approximately 1½ minutes or until a skin forms. Scoop out using a slotted spoon, then rinse in a clean water bath. Scoop out again and drain on paper towel. You will need 30 spheres. Serve immediately.

PRESENTATION

Arrange the venison tartare on 6 serving plates. Carefully spoon the wasabi spheres over the top and garnish with the croûtons. Serves 6.

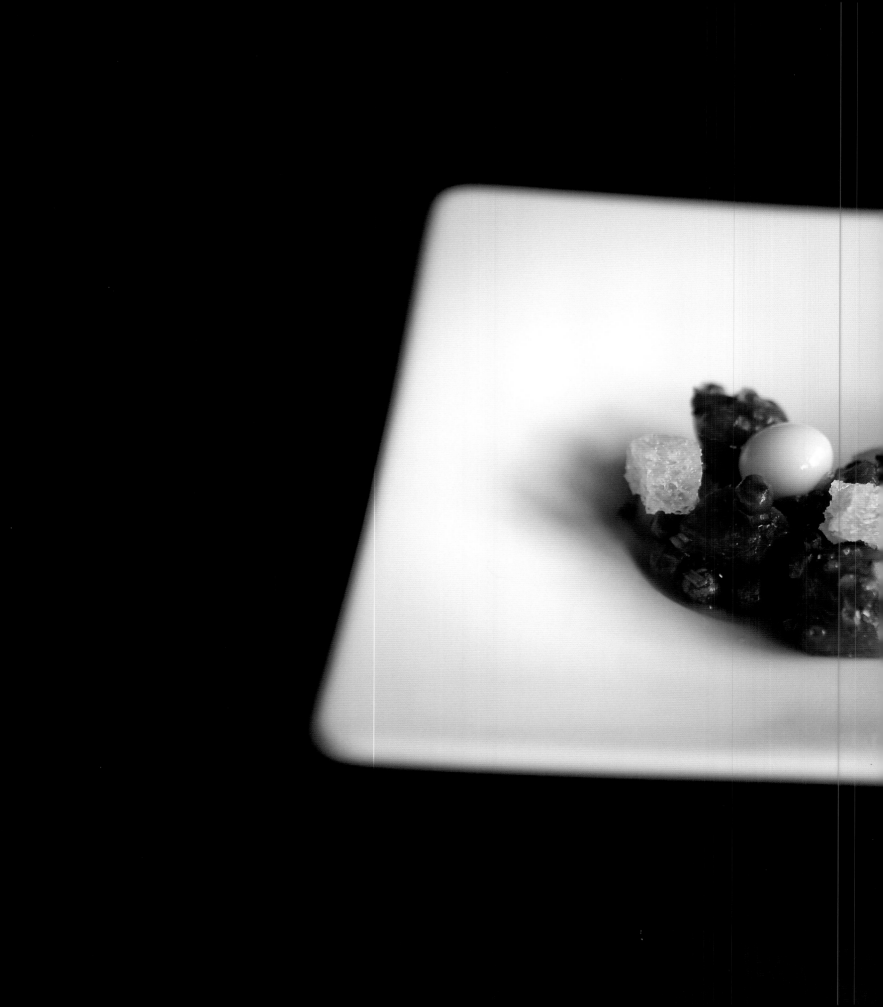

At the restaurant, we use a thermoregulator to maintain the water temperature for this recipe. The temperature given, 63°C (145°F), is quite specific and should not vary by more than 2°C (36°F) on either side. The reason for this is that at this temperature both the egg white and yolk cook at the same rate. The result is a creamy textured egg with an even consistency throughout.

SOFT FREE-RANGE EGG WITH ALMOND BREAD CRUNCH AND SHERRY CARAMEL

ALMOND BREAD CRUNCH

2 x 2 cm (¾ inch) thick sourdough bread slices
50 g (1¾ oz/⅓ cup) blanched almonds, toasted
sea salt flakes

Preheat the oven to 160°C (315°F/Gas 2–3). Bake the bread for 8 minutes or until completely dry and crisp. Allow to cool. Very thinly slice lengthways with a sharp knife — the bread should shatter into small pieces.

Thinly slice the almonds lengthways. Combine with the breadcrumbs and season with the salt. Set aside.

This can be made 1 day in advance and stored in an airtight container.

SHERRY CARAMEL

30 ml (1 fl oz) honey
30 ml (1 fl oz) sherry vinegar

Place the honey and vinegar in a small saucepan and bring to the boil. Reduce the heat to medium and continue to cook for 8–10 minutes or until the mixture reaches 110–112°C (230–234°F) and is a caramel. Set aside.

This can be made 1 day in advance and stored in an airtight container in the fridge.

ORANGE OIL

2 oranges
30 ml (1 fl oz) olive oil

Using a microplane grater, finely grate the zest of the oranges into a bowl, making sure you catch all the oils. Discard the oranges. Transfer the zest to an airtight container, making sure to scrape up the oils. Cover with the oil and leave in a warm place for 1 hour to infuse.

Strain through a fine sieve, pressing as much oil out of the zest as possible. Discard the zest and set the orange oil aside.

EGG

6 free-range eggs

Heat a saucepan of water to 63°C (145°F). Gently place the eggs into the pan and cook for 1½ hours. Using a slotted spoon, remove the eggs. Use the back of a small knife to crack each one open — be careful as you don't want to break the yolks. Serve immediately.

PRESENTATION

sea salt and freshly ground black pepper
finely chopped dill leaves, for garnish

Drizzle some sherry caramel in the bases of 6 small bowls and spoon the almond bread crunch on top. Carefully place an egg on top and season with salt and pepper. Drizzle with the orange oil and garnish with the dill. Serves 6.

MUSSELS AND CLAMS WITH SAFFRON SOFRITO

SAFFRON SOFRITO

100 ml (3½ fl oz) vegetable oil
1 red capsicum (pepper)
50 ml (1¾ fl oz) olive oil
8 eschalots (French shallots), finely diced
2 garlic cloves
2 long red chillies, seeds removed and thinly sliced
2 g (1/16 oz) saffron threads
40 ml (1¼ fl oz) white wine
sea salt and freshly ground black pepper

Heat the vegetable oil in a small frying pan over medium–high heat. Add the whole capsicum and cook, turning occasionally, for about 3 minutes or until blistered all over. Cool, then peel and remove the seeds. Cut into 5 mm (¼ inch) dice and set aside.

Heat the olive oil in a saucepan over low heat. Add the eschalot and cook for 10 minutes or until translucent. Add the garlic, chilli and capsicum and cook, stirring often, for about 1 hour or until the moisture is evaporated — take care that the mixture does not stick to the base of the pan.

Soak the saffron in the wine for 30 minutes. Add the saffron mixture to the pan and cook for 2–3 minutes or until the wine is evaporated. Season with salt and pepper.

MUSSELS AND CLAMS

300 ml (10½ fl oz) white wine
2 fresh bay leaves
4 sprigs thyme
10 g (⅓ oz) black peppercorns
500 g (1 lb 2 oz) black mussels, scrubbed
    and debearded
500 g (1 lb 2 oz) clams (vongole), purged and drained
1 quantity saffron sofrito

Place half of each of the wine, bay leaf, thyme and peppercorns in a saucepan and bring to the boil. Add the mussels and cover with a glass lid. As the mussels open, remove them from the pan and set aside. Discard the cooking liquid.

Repeat with the clams and remaining half of the ingredients.

Remove the mussels and clams from their shells and stir into the saffron sofrito. Serve immediately.

LOTUS ROOT CRISPS

200 g (7 oz) fresh lotus root (about ½ small), peeled
100 ml (3½ fl oz) vegetable oil
sea salt flakes

Using a mandolin, slice the lotus root widthways into 1 mm (1/32 inch) thick slices. Heat the oil in a small saucepan to 180°C (350°F). Cook the lotus root for about 1 minute or until golden and crisp. Remove and drain on paper towel. Season with salt and set aside.

PRESENTATION

rocket (arugula) shoots, for garnish

Spoon the mussels, clams and sofrito onto 6 plates. Garnish with the lotus root crisps and rocket shoots. Serves 6.

CHICKPEA CHIPS WITH GARLIC CUSTARD

GARLIC CUSTARD

500 g (1 lb 2 oz) roasted garlic purée (see page 25)
200 ml (7 fl oz) pouring (single) cream
200 g (7 oz/2 cups) finely grated parmesan
9 eggs, lightly beaten
10 g (⅓ oz) sea salt flakes

Preheat the oven to 150°C (300°F/Gas 2).

Heat the roasted garlic purée to 60°C (140°F) in a small saucepan. Bring the cream and parmesan to the boil in a separate small saucepan.

Place the beaten egg and salt in a bowl and, using a stick blender, aerate slightly for 1 minute. Add the roasted garlic purée and cream mixture and blend until well combined. Pass through a fine sieve into a 30 x 20 x 4 cm (12 x 8 x 1½ inch) baking dish.

Bake for 20 minutes or until the mixture is firm. Cool to room temperature, then refrigerate until chilled.

To serve, transfer the mixture to an upright blender and blend until smooth and thick. Serve immediately.

CHICKPEA CHIPS

1 litre (35 fl oz/4 cups) milk
3 teaspoons olive oil
15 g (½ oz) unsalted butter
15 g (½ oz) sea salt flakes
5 g (⅙ oz) fennel seeds, ground
250 g (9 oz/2¼ cups) chickpea flour (besan)
20 g (¾ oz) fine semolina
vegetable oil, for deep-frying

Line a 30 x 20 x 4 cm (12 x 8 x 1½ inch) metal tray with baking paper.

Place the milk, olive oil, butter, salt and ground fennel in a saucepan over medium–high heat and bring to the boil. While whisking continuously, gradually add the chickpea flour until smooth and thick. Pour into the lined tray, cool to room temperature, then refrigerate until chilled.

Remove from the tray and cut into 8 x 1.5 cm (3¼ x ⅝ inch) chips. You will need 54 chips. Roll in the semolina to coat, shaking off any excess.

Heat the vegetable oil to 175°C (347°F) in a deep saucepan or deep-fryer. Fry the chips until golden all over. Season with salt and serve immediately.

PRESENTATION

You will need 9 chickpea chips per serve. Arrange the chips in a lattice on a plate. Using 2 tablespoons, place a quenelle of garlic custard alongside. Serves 6.

CRISP SPICED CHICKEN WITH AÏOLI

CRISP SPICED CHICKEN

2 chicken breast fillets (about 400 g/14 oz in total)
20 ml (⅔ fl oz) fish sauce, approximately
300 g (10½ oz/1¾ cups) tapioca flour
vegetable oil, for deep-frying
20 g (⅔ oz) sumac

Cut each chicken breast widthways into 4 pieces and place between freezer film. Flatten with a meat mallet until 2–3 mm (1/16–⅛ inch) thick. Remove the freezer film and thinly slice the chicken with a sharp knife — it should tear apart and resemble coarse mince. Place in a bowl and add enough fish sauce to lightly coat. Add the flour and, using your fingers, toss until coated and separated into clumps, then place in a sieve and shake to remove excess flour.

Heat the oil in a large deep saucepan or deep-fryer to 180°C (350°F). Deep-fry the chicken, turning regularly with tongs or shaking the fryer basket, for 1 minute or until golden and crisp. Remove and drain on paper towel. While hot, toss in sumac. Serve immediately.

PRESENTATION

6 small paper cones
1 quantity aïoli (see page 24)

Fill the paper cones with the spiced chicken and serve the aïoli on the side. Serves 6.

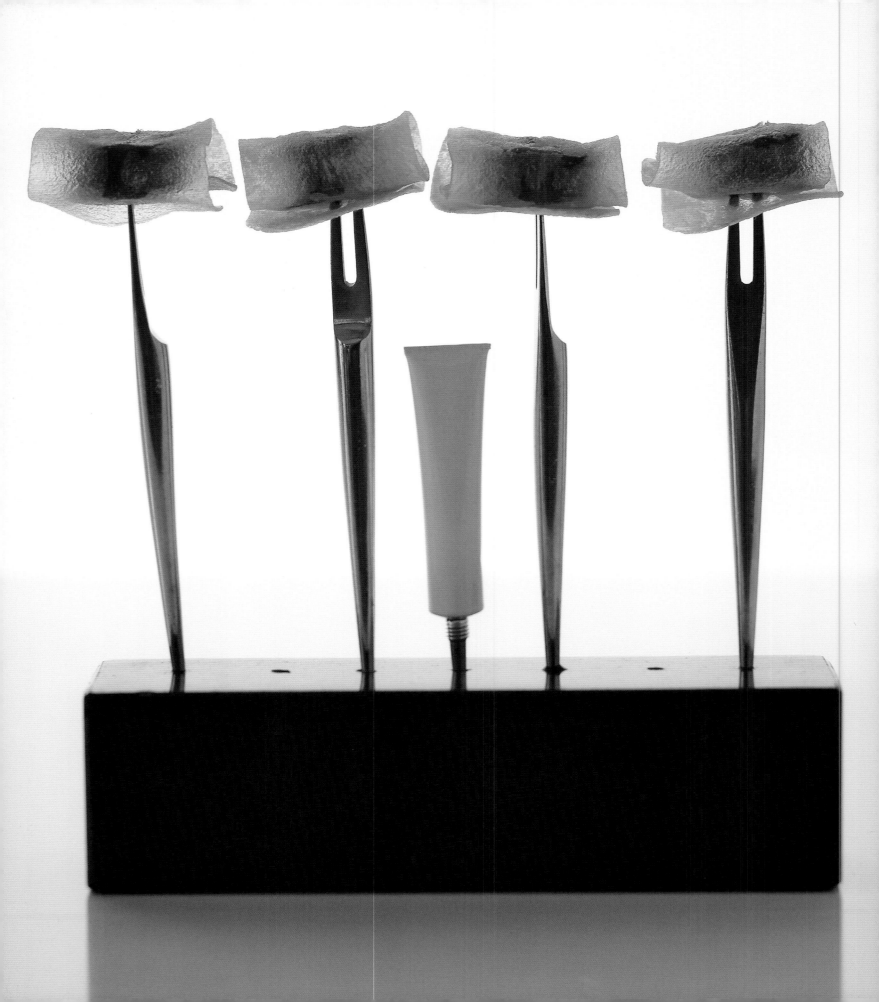

CRISP POTATO AND CHORIZO

HARISSA SPICE MIX

1 cinnamon stick
20 g (⅔ oz) coriander seeds
20 g (⅔ oz) cumin seeds
10 g (⅓ oz) fennel seeds
5 g (⅙ oz) black peppercorns

Preheat the oven to 160°C (315°F/Gas 2–3). Roast the spices for 5 minutes. Remove and allow to cool. Place in a spice grinder and grind to a fine powder, then pass through a fine sieve, discarding the solids.

This can be stored in an airtight container for up to 2 weeks.

HARISSA

5 red capsicums (peppers), seeds removed
150 ml (5 fl oz) vegetable oil
2 long red chillies, seeds removed
1 birds-eye chilli, halved
4 garlic cloves
3 star anise
2 fresh bay leaves
2 tablespoons harissa spice mix
sea salt flakes
20 ml (⅔ fl oz) sherry vinegar, or to taste

Dice the capsicums into 2.5 cm (1 inch) cubes. Heat the oil in a large heavy-based frying pan over medium heat. Cook the capsicum, stirring regularly, for 20 minutes. Add the chillies, garlic, star anise and bay leaves. Cook for another 10 minutes, then reduce the heat to low and simmer for 1½ hours. Stir in the spice mix.

Transfer the mixture to an upright blender and blend until smooth, then pass through a drum sieve (tamis). Season with the salt and vinegar. Place the harissa in a piping bag fitted with a 2 mm (1/16 inch) plain nozzle and refrigerate until ready to serve.

CHORIZO AND POTATO

200 g (7 oz) desiree potato
320 g (11¼ oz) chorizo sausage
200 ml (7 fl oz) vegetable oil
sea salt and freshly ground black pepper

Using a mandolin, thinly slice the potato lengthways into 1 mm (1/32 inch) thick slices. Cut the chorizo into 7 mm (⅜ inch) thick slices. Wrap a slice of potato the entire way around a piece of chorizo and secure with a toothpick. Repeat with the remaining potato and chorizo.

Heat the oil in a large deep frying pan to 170°C (325°F) and shallow-fry the chorizo and potato parcels until golden and crisp. Remove using tongs and drain on paper towel. Serve immediately.

PRESENTATION

At the restaurant we serve the chorizo and potato parcels on small forks and the harissa in a tube. I suggest you pipe a line of harissa onto 6 plates and arrange the chorizo and potato parcels on top. Spike each with a toothpick to serve. Serves 6.

PIMENTOS DE PADRÓN WITH SHERRY VINEGAR AND GARLIC

CRISP GARLIC

2 garlic cloves, thinly sliced lengthways using a mandolin
½ teaspoon sea salt flakes
40 ml (1¼ fl oz) vegetable oil

Combine the garlic with the salt in a bowl and set aside for 10 minutes to draw out the moisture, then rinse off the salt and pat dry with paper towel. Heat the oil in a small frying pan over medium heat. Cook the garlic for 3 minutes or until golden and crisp. Remove from the pan and drain on paper towel. Set aside.

PIMENTOS DE PADRÓN

30 ml (1 fl oz) extra virgin olive oil
150 g (5½ oz) pimentos de Padrón (see Note)
3 garlic cloves, thinly sliced crossways using a mandolin
20 ml (⅔ fl oz) sherry vinegar

Heat the oil in a large frying pan over high heat. Add the pimentos and cook, tossing often, until evenly blistered and scorched. Add the garlic and cook until golden. Remove the pan from the heat and deglaze with the vinegar. Serve immediately.

NOTE Pimentos de Padrón are a pepper originating from Galicia in Spain. Approximately only 1 in 10 are hot and they're in season for only 2 months of the year during summer. They're available from select greengrocers.

PRESENTATION

Place the pimentos in a serving bowl, drizzle over the pan juices and garnish with the crisp garlic. Serves 6.

ENTRÉES

Starters for me are all about flavour. They are a precursor of what is to come, so it is important that they have maximum flavour. The smaller portions of entrées allow me to be playful with ingredients and textures. The black sesame and pea fondant with goat's curd and snow peas (see page 98) is a good example. Despite their small serving size, entrées often have a big punch line, determining the pace of the rest of the meal.

BOUDIN NOIR WITH YABBIES, MANDARIN AND ALMOND

BOUDIN NOIR

180 g (6½ oz) pork back fat
1 large onion, diced
2 teaspoons quatre épices (four spice)
10 g (⅓ oz) sea salt flakes
100 ml (3½ fl oz) pouring (single) cream
20 g (⅔ oz) panko breadcrumbs (see Notes)
350 ml (12 fl oz) pig's blood (see Notes)

Preheat the oven to 140°C (275°F/Gas 1). Dice the fat into small pieces. Place half in a frying pan over medium heat and cook until rendered. Add the onion, quatre épices and salt and cook for 5 minutes. Remove from the heat and allow to cool slightly. Stir through the cream, breadcrumbs and remaining diced fat. Stir through the pig's blood.

Pour into a 30 x 25 x 6 cm (12 x 10 x 2½ inch) tray lined with baking paper. Place in a bain-marie and bake for 1 hour. Remove from the oven and bain-marie and allow to cool. Remove the boudin noir from the tray and cut into 6 equal portions. Reheat in the oven before serving.

NOTES Panko breadcrumbs are Japanese breadcrumbs, available from Asian grocers. You can substitute fresh breadcrumbs. You can get pig's blood from butchers but you will need to order it in advance.

MANDARIN PURÉE

8–10 mandarins
3 g (¹⁄₁₀ oz) agar agar
30 ml (1 fl oz) olive oil
sea salt flakes

Peel the mandarins, reserving the peel. Remove the seeds and place the flesh in an upright blender and blend until smooth. Strain through a fine sieve. Measure 600 ml (21 fl oz) juice and place in a small saucepan over medium heat. Cook for 10 minutes or until reduced by half. Add the agar agar and cook for 1 minute. Refrigerate for 1 hour or until set.

Meanwhile, remove the pith from the peel. Bring a small saucepan of water to the boil and blanch the peel for 1 minute. Drain, refresh in iced water and drain again.

Repeat blanching, refreshing and draining 2 more times, then cut the peel into small pieces.

Place the chilled mandarin mixture in an upright blender with the peel and oil and blend until smooth. Season with salt, then pass through a fine sieve. Set aside.

YABBIES

18 live yabbies
50 g (1¾ oz) unsalted butter

Bring a large saucepan of water to the boil. Cook the yabbies for 1 minute. Drain and refresh in iced water, then drain again. Remove the tail meat, discarding the shells and claws. Melt the butter in a large frying pan over medium heat and cook the yabbies for 2 minutes. Remove from the pan and keep warm. Reserve the pan juices.

YABBIE SALAD

1 mandarin
1 punnet coriander (cilantro) shoots, trimmed
7 g (¼ oz) coriander seeds, toasted
10 g (⅓ oz) blanched almonds, toasted
    and halved
sea salt and freshly ground white pepper
1 quantity yabbies and reserved pan juices
2 teaspoons lemon juice

Peel and segment the mandarin. Halve each segment, place in a bowl with the coriander shoots, coriander seeds and almonds and season with salt and pepper. Add the yabbies and dress with the lemon juice and reserved pan juices. Serve immediately.

PRESENTATION

Place a quenelle of mandarin purée on one side of 6 plates. Position the boudin noir opposite it. Place 2 yabbies on top of the boudin and garnish the rest of the plate with more of the yabbie salad. Serves 6.

KINGFISH MARINATED IN SQUID INK WITH PERFUMED FRUIT AND COCONUT

PERFUMED FRUIT

1 semi-ripe mango, peeled and seed removed
1 nashi pear, peeled, halved and core removed
1 apple, peeled, halved and core removed
1 yellow peach, halved and stone removed
1 ml (1/32 fl oz) bergamot essence (see Note)
3 teaspoons olive oil

Dice the fruit into 5 mm (1/4 inch) cubes and combine. Dress with the bergamot essence and oil and set aside.

This can be made up to 2 hours in advance.

NOTE It's important to use food-grade bergamot essence, available from aromatherapy shops.

COCONUT PURÉE

250 ml (9 fl oz/1 cup) Kara coconut cream
2 g (1/16 oz) agar agar

Place 200 ml (7 fl oz) coconut cream and the agar agar in a small saucepan and bring to the boil, stirring continuously, then reduce the heat to low and simmer for 3 minutes, still stirring. Pour into a metal bowl and refrigerate for 1 hour or until set.

Transfer to an upright blender, add the remaining coconut cream and blend until smooth. Pass through a fine sieve. Set aside.

KINGFISH

40 ml (1¼ fl oz) squid ink
20 ml (⅔ fl oz) olive oil
sea salt flakes
500 g (1 lb 2 oz) piece of kingfish loin (see Note)

Heat a large saucepan of water to 67°C (153°F).

Whisk together the squid ink, oil and a pinch of salt in a bowl. Cut the kingfish widthways into 6 equal portions, add to the squid ink mixture and rub to coat well.

Place each portion in a small vacuum-seal or zip-lock bag. Follow the Masterclass on sous-vide cooking (see page 16) and cook the fish for 3 minutes.

Remove the kingfish from the bags. Trim the sides to neaten the shape — the kingfish should be quite rare in the middle. Set aside.

NOTE The loin is from the top half of a kingfish fillet.

SCALLOPS

20 ml (⅔ fl oz) vegetable oil
6 scallops, roe removed

Heat the oil in a small frying pan over high heat. Sear the scallops on one side for 1 minute, then turn and sear the other side for 20 seconds. Remove from the pan and keep warm.

PRESENTATION

edible flowers (such as viola, rosemary or fruit salad), for garnish

Place the perfumed fruit in the centre of 6 plates. Place a piece of kingfish next to the fruit and a scallop on the other side of the plate. Spoon the coconut purée next to the kingfish and garnish with the flowers. Serves 6.

YELLOWFIN TUNA WITH RED PEPPER CRUMBS, YOGHURT AND ANCHOVY

RED PEPPER CRUMBS

2 red peppers (capsicums)
1 tomato
40 ml (1¼ fl oz) olive oil
1 onion, diced
1 long red chilli, seeds removed and sliced
2 garlic cloves, sliced
40 g (1¼ oz) ground almonds (almond meal)

Rub the peppers and tomato with half of the oil and roast for 20 minutes or until blistered, then transfer to a bowl and cover with plastic wrap. When cool enough to handle, remove the skins and dice the flesh.

Place the onion, chilli, garlic and remaining oil in a saucepan over medium heat and cook for 10 minutes or until softened. Add the pepper and tomato, reduce the heat to low and cook for 10 minutes. Transfer to a food processor and process until smooth.

Spread over a non-stick baking mat and place on a baking tray. Dry in a dehydrator at 80°C (176°F) for 1 hour. Alternatively, place in the oven on the lowest temperature and leave until completely dry. Remove and refrigerate until chilled.

Place in a food processor along with the ground almonds and process until small crumbs form.

This can be made 1 day in advance and stored in an airtight container in the fridge.

RED PEPPER JELLY

1 teaspoon Sichuan peppercorns
2 g (¹⁄₁₆ oz) coriander seeds
½ whole allspice
1 fresh bay leaf
400 ml (14 fl oz) red pepper (capsicum) juice
    (about 2 peppers)
100 ml (3½ fl oz) blood orange juice (about 2 oranges)
sea salt flakes
caster (superfine) sugar, to taste
2 sheets gelatine, titanium strength
2 teaspoons olive oil

Preheat the oven to 180°C (350°F/Gas 4). Roast the spices and bay leaf for 3–4 minutes.

Place the red pepper and orange juices in a saucepan and bring to the boil, skimming the scum from the surface regularly. Add the roasted spices and simmer for 8 minutes or until reduced to 300 ml (10½ fl oz), skimming regularly. Remove from the heat and set aside for 30 minutes to infuse. Season with salt and sugar. Pass through a fine sieve.

Soak the gelatine in cold water for 5 minutes or until softened, then squeeze to remove the excess water. Add the gelatine to the juice mixture, stirring to dissolve. Transfer to a container and refrigerate for 1 hour or until set.

This can be made 1 day in advance. When ready to serve, add the oil and mix in using a fork, breaking up the jelly. Set aside. This makes more than you will need.

YOGHURT

250 g (9 oz/1 cup) plain yoghurt
4.5 g (¹⁄₂₅ oz) methylcellulose
1.5 g (¹⁄₂₀ oz) xanthan gum
2 sheets gelatine, titanium strength

Place the yoghurt, methylcellulose, xanthan gum and 200 ml (7 fl oz) water in an upright blender and mix until well combined. Transfer to a plastic container, place in the freezer and chill until 1–4°C (34–39°F). Place in the bowl of an electric mixer.

Soften the gelatine in cold water for 5 minutes, then squeeze to remove the excess water. Place the gelatine in a small saucepan with 2 teaspoons of water and place over medium heat. Stir to dissolve the gelatine, then add to the yoghurt mixture and whisk for 5 minutes or until combined. Place a sheet of plastic wrap on a work surface. Place the mixture in the middle of the plastic, roll into a 3 cm (1¼ inch) cylinder, then tie the ends to secure. Refrigerate for 1 hour or until set.

This can be made 1 day in advance. When ready to serve, bring the yoghurt to room temperature, remove the plastic wrap and cut the yoghurt into six 3 cm (1¼ inch) pieces. This will make more than you will need.

SPICE MIX

25 g (⅘ oz) coriander seeds
15 g (½ oz) black peppercorns
20 g (¾ oz) cardamom seeds
½ cinnamon stick
½ star anise
7 g (¼ oz) caster (superfine) sugar

Preheat the oven to 170°C (325°F/Gas 3). Roast the spices for 8 minutes. Transfer to a spice grinder and finely grind. Combine with the sugar, then pass through a fine sieve. Set aside.

SPICED CAULIFLOWER

¾ head cauliflower (about 600 g/1 lb 5 oz)
1 quantity spice mix
sea salt flakes

Grate the cauliflower, tops only, so it resembles couscous. Discard the stem. Place the cauliflower in a bowl and mix through the spice mix. Season with salt and set aside.

CAULIFLOWER PURÉE

¼ head cauliflower (about 200 g/7 oz)
100 ml (3½ fl oz) milk
sea salt and freshly ground black pepper

Thinly slice the cauliflower, discarding the stem. Place in a saucepan with the milk, season with salt and pepper and cover with a cartouche. Cook over medium heat for 12 minutes or until tender. Transfer to an upright blender and blend until smooth. Transfer to a piping bag fitted with a 3 mm (⅛ inch) plain nozzle and refrigerate until required.

YELLOWFIN TUNA

6 x 80 g (2¾ oz) pieces of yellowfin tuna loin
sea salt flakes
40 ml (1¼ fl oz) olive oil

Season the tuna with salt. Heat the oil in a frying pan over medium heat. Sear the tuna for 1 minute each side. Set aside and keep warm.

PRESENTATION

6 Ortiz anchovy fillets (see Note)
mustard cress shoots, for garnish

Top each piece of tuna with the spiced cauliflower. Place the red pepper crumbs in a small pile on 6 plates. Place the tuna on top and spoon red pepper jelly around the plate. Pipe dots of cauliflower purée around the plate. Arrange a piece of yoghurt next to the tuna and lay over an anchovy. Garnish with the mustard cress shoots. Serves 6.

NOTE These top-quality Spanish anchovies are available from gourmet food stores.

ALMOND GAZPACHO WITH MILK CRISP AND OYSTER

MILK CRISP

100 ml (3½ fl oz) skim milk
10 g (⅓ oz) powdered skim milk
10 g (⅓ oz) powdered egg white (see Note)
5 g (⅙ oz) caster (superfine) sugar

Place all the ingredients in a bowl. Using an electric beater, beat on medium speed until firm peaks form. Place in a piping bag fitted with a 4 mm (¼ inch) plain nozzle and pipe lengths onto a non-stick baking mat. Place on a baking tray and dry in a dehydrator at 60°C (140°F) for 6 hours. Alternatively, place in the oven on the lowest temperature and leave until completely dry. Break into small lengths. Set aside.

These can be made 1 day in advance and stored in an airtight container.

NOTE **Powdered egg white is available from health food stores.**

ALMOND GAZPACHO

200 ml (7 fl oz) almond oil
20 ml (⅔ fl oz) sherry vinegar
100 g (3½ oz/⅔ cup) blanched almonds
½ garlic clove
1 g (¹⁄₃₂ oz) xanthan gum
sea salt flakes

Place all the ingredients and 250 ml (9 fl oz/1 cup) water in an upright blender and blend until smooth. Season with salt. Pass through a fine sieve. Transfer to a cream canister and charge twice. Set aside.

PRESENTATION

6 freshly shucked Kumamoto-style Pacific oysters (see Notes)
20 ml (⅔ fl oz) almond oil
20 g (⅔ oz) Avruga (see Notes)
borage flowers, for garnish

Cover the bases of 6 bowls with the almond gazpacho. Place an oyster in the centre, drizzle over the almond oil and place a dollop of Avruga alongside. Top with 6 pieces of milk crisp and garnish with the flowers. Serves 6.

NOTES **Kumamoto-style Pacific oysters are small plump creamy oysters. They're also called 'virgin' oysters as they are harvested before they have spawned. Avruga is herring roe, available from select fishmongers.**

ROASTED PIGEON WITH PISTACHIO, ORANGE TAPIOCA AND DRIED FRUIT PASTE

DRIED FRUIT PASTE

50 g (1¾ oz) dried prunes, pitted
50 g (1¾ oz) dried figs
50 g (1¾ oz) dried apricots
50 g (1¾ oz) dried dates
3 g (¹⁄₁₀ oz) agar agar

Place the dried fruit and 400 ml (14 fl oz) water in a saucepan and bring to the boil. Reduce the heat to medium and simmer for 15 minutes or until broken down, adding extra water, if necessary, to keep the fruit just covered. Transfer to an upright blender and blend until smooth. Return to the pan and place over medium heat. Add the agar agar and cook, stirring occasionally, until it reaches 90°C (194°F). Transfer to a small container and refrigerate for 1½ hours or until set. This can be made 1 day in advance.

PISTACHIO PURÉE

50 ml (1¾ fl oz) olive oil
20 ml (⅔ fl oz) vegetable oil
100 g (3½ oz/¾ cup) Iranian pistachio kernels
2 garlic cloves, finely chopped
finely grated zest of 1 orange

Place all the ingredients and 40 ml (1¼ fl oz) water in an upright blender and blend until smooth. Set aside.

This can be made 1 day in advance and stored in the fridge in an airtight container.

ORANGE TAPIOCA

750 ml (26 fl oz/3 cups) freshly squeezed orange juice (about 8 oranges)
100 g (3½ oz) small tapioca pearls (see Note)
sea salt and freshly ground black pepper

Place the tapioca and 500 ml (17 fl oz/2 cups) juice in a saucepan and bring to the boil. Reduce to a simmer and, while stirring continuously, add 250 ml (9 fl oz/1 cup) water. Continue to cook, stirring occasionally, for about 25 minutes or until the tapioca is transparent.

Place the remaining juice in a small saucepan over medium heat and simmer for about 10 minutes or until reduced by two-thirds to a thick glaze. Add to the tapioca and season with salt and pepper. Set aside and keep warm.

NOTE Tapioca pearls are available from Asian grocers.

ROASTED PIGEON

3 pigeons
sea salt flakes and freshly ground black pepper
1 head garlic, cloves separated and sliced
1 bunch (20 g/¾ oz) thyme
1 fresh bay leaf
olive oil
40 g (1½ oz) Dijon mustard
100 g (3½ oz/¾ cup) Iranian pistachio kernels

Remove the pigeon legs from the body by cutting through the thigh joint. Place the legs on a tray, sprinkle with ½ teaspoon salt, the garlic and herbs, then cover and refrigerate for 1 hour. Remove the breast fillets from the bone and refrigerate until required.

Preheat the oven to 150°C (300°F/Gas 2). Remove the legs from the fridge, rinse off the salt and pat dry with paper towel. Place in a snug-fitting roasting tray and pour in enough oil to cover. Bake for 1 hour, then remove from the oven and allow to cool in the oil. Once cool, pick the meat from the bones, discarding the skin and bones. Season the meat with the mustard, salt and pepper. Press the meat into a 10 cm (4 inch) square container and refrigerate for 3–4 hours or until chilled.

When ready to serve, preheat the oven to 140°C (275°F/Gas 1). Turn the chilled leg meat out and cut into 2.5 cm (1 inch) cubes. You will need 18 cubes. Place on a baking tray lined with baking paper, drizzle with oil and warm in the oven for 5 minutes. Using a microplane grater, grate the pistachios. Remove the meat from the oven and coat with the grated pistachio. Set aside and keep warm.

Meanwhile, season the breast fillets with salt. Heat 2 teaspoons of oil in an ovenproof frying pan over medium heat and sear the breasts until golden on both sides, then roast for 3 minutes — they should be quite pink in the middle. Rest in a warm place until ready to serve. Just before serving, carve each breast fillet in half.

PRESENTATION

Spread a layer of pistachio purée across 6 plates. Using 2 hot teaspoons, place 2 quenelles of dried fruit paste on each plate. Place 3 dollops of orange tapioca around each plate and top with a cube of leg meat. Position 2 pieces of breast fillet on opposing sides of the plate. Serves 6.

BASIL PUDDING WITH SWEETCORN AND ZUCCHINI FLOWER SALAD

BASIL WATER

⅔ bunch (60 g/2¼ oz) basil, leaves picked
sea salt flakes

Blanch the basil in lightly salted boiling for 1 minute. Drain and refresh in iced water, then drain again and cool. Transfer to an upright blender, add 300 ml (10½ fl oz) water and blend until smooth. Pass through a fine sieve, discarding the solids. Set aside.

This can be made 1 day in advance and stored in an airtight container in the fridge.

BASIL PUDDING

300 ml (10½ fl oz) basil water
1 g (¹⁄₃₂ oz) methylcellulose
60 g (2¼ oz) basil seeds (see Note)

Place 100 ml (3½ fl oz) basil water and the methylcellulose in a blender and blend until combined. Transfer to a container, place in the freezer and chill to 1–4°C (34–39°F).

Place the basil seeds and remaining basil water in a small bowl and allow to stand until the seeds have absorbed all of the water.

Stir the soaked basil seeds into the chilled basil water mixture. Divide into 10 g (⅓ oz) balls. You will need 18 balls. Place each in the centre of a 30 cm (12 inch) square piece of plastic wrap. Take all 4 corners of the plastic wrap and twist together to form a tight ball. Tie off tightly to secure.

These can be made up to 1 day in advance and refrigerated. When ready to serve, poach the balls in boiling water for 3 minutes or until set. Scoop out and remove the plastic wrap. Set aside.

NOTE Basil seeds are available from Asian grocers.

SWEETCORN PURÉE

4 cobs sweetcorn

Remove the husks from the corn and, using a large sharp knife, cut off the kernels as close as possible to the cobs. Juice the kernels in a juicer. Transfer the juice to a double boiler over simmering water and cook for 5–10 minutes or until thick, silky and smooth. Pass through a fine sieve. Set aside and keep warm.

This can be made up to 1 day in advance and stored in an airtight container in the fridge. Reheat before serving.

GOAT'S CURD DRESSING

120 g (4¼ oz) goat's curd
40 ml (1¼ fl oz) extra virgin olive oil
freshly ground white pepper
2 teaspoons lemon juice

Place the goat's curd and oil in an upright blender and blend until smooth. Season with pepper and lemon juice. Transfer to a piping bag fitted with a 2 mm (¹⁄₁₆ inch) plain nozzle and set aside.

SOY BEANS

200 g (7 oz) frozen soy (edamame) beans, thawed and podded
20 ml (⅔ fl oz) goat's curd dressing
2 teaspoons olive oil

Place all the ingredients in a small bowl and stir to coat the soy beans well. Set aside.

ZUCCHINI

2 large zucchini (courgettes)
4 spears green asparagus, trimmed
3 zucchini flowers (with baby zucchini attached)
2 sprigs dill, leaves picked
20 ml (⅔ fl oz) goat's curd dressing
1 teaspoon extra virgin olive oil
sea salt and freshly ground black pepper

Peel the zucchini and, using a mandolin, slice lengthways into 1 mm (¹⁄₃₂ inch) thick slices, discarding the middle part with the seeds. You will need 9 slices. Set aside.

Slice the asparagus lengthways into 1 mm (¹⁄₃₂ inch) thick slices. Remove the flowers from the baby zucchini and set aside for garnish. Slice the baby zucchini lengthways into 1 mm (¹⁄₃₂ inch) thick slices. Roughly chop the dill and combine with the asparagus and baby zucchini and half of the goat's curd dressing.

Lay the zucchini slices vertically on a work surface. Neatly place the salad across each slice, allowing it to extend about 2 cm (¾ inch) either side of the slice. Roll each up tightly to form cylinders, then halve widthways. Serve immediately.

PRESENTATION

Spoon the sweetcorn purée onto 6 plates. Place 3 basil balls on the plate and stand a zucchini cylinder alongside each one. Garnish with the zucchini flower petals and place small piles of soy beans around the plate. Pipe dots of the goat's curd dressing on the plate to finish. Serves 6.

BLACK SESAME AND PEA FONDANT WITH GOAT'S CURD AND SNOW PEAS

BLACK SESAME PURÉE

½ onion, diced
2 garlic cloves, thinly sliced
15 g (½ oz) ginger, thinly sliced
20 ml (⅔ fl oz) vegetable oil
10 g (⅓ oz) sea salt flakes
250 g (9 oz/1⅔ cups) black sesame seeds
40 ml (1¼ fl oz) pomegranate molasses
3.5 g (⅛ oz) ground star anise
3.5 g (⅛ oz) ground fennel
0.5 g cayenne pepper
6 g (⅕ oz) caster (superfine) sugar
5 g (⅙ oz) methylcellulose
1.5 g (¹⁄₂₀ oz) xanthan gum
1 teaspoon lemon juice

Place the onion, garlic, ginger, oil and 2 g (¹⁄₁₆ oz) salt in a saucepan over medium heat and cook for 5 minutes. Add the sesame seeds and 1.1 litres (38½ fl oz) water and bring to the boil. Reduce the heat to low and simmer for 30 minutes. Remove from the heat and infuse for 10 minutes, then strain, reserving the liquid and seeds. Set aside 125 ml (4 fl oz/½ cup) liquid to make the black sesame glass.

Blend the seeds and remaining liquid, in two equal batches, in an upright blender until smooth. Pass through a fine sieve, discarding the solids.

Return both strained batches to the blender and, with the motor running, add the pomegranate molasses, spices, sugar, methylcellulose and xanthan gum. Add the lemon juice and remaining salt and blend until well combined. Transfer to a piping bag fitted with a 5 mm (¼ inch) plain nozzle, then place in the freezer and chill until 1–4°C (34–39°F). Once chilled, refrigerate until required.

BLACK SESAME GLASS

125 ml (4 fl oz/½ cup) black sesame seed liquid
    (reserved from black sesame purée)
30 g (1 oz) isomalt
8 g (⁷⁄₂₅ oz) maltodextrin
2 g (¹⁄₁₆ oz) xanthan gum

Place all the ingredients in a bowl and blend together using a stick blender. Transfer to a small saucepan and heat to 80°C (176°F). Spread evenly over a non-stick baking mat to 2 mm (¹⁄₁₆ inch) thick and place on a baking tray. Dry in a dehydrator at 60°C (140°F) for 1½ hours. Alternatively, place in the oven on the lowest temperature and leave until completely dry. Cut the black sesame glass into 3 x 2 cm (1¼ x ¾ inch) rectangles. Set aside.

This can be made 1 day in advance and stored in an airtight container.

PEA PURÉE

½ onion, diced
2 small garlic cloves, sliced
2 teaspoons olive oil
500 g (1 lb 2 oz) podded green peas
    (about 1.2 kg/2 lb 10 oz unpodded)

Place the onion, garlic and oil in a saucepan over medium heat and cook for 3 minutes or until softened. Add 1 litre (35 fl oz/4 cups) water and bring to the boil. Add the peas and cook for 1½ minutes. Strain, reserving the liquid and peas. Place the peas in an upright blender with enough reserved cooking liquid to come one-quarter of the way up the peas and blend until smooth. Pass through a fine sieve. Divide into 3 x 150 ml (5 fl oz) portions and place in separate bowls. Set aside 2 portions to make the pea crumbs and pea gel. Place the remaining portion in a piping bag fitted with a 2 mm (¹⁄₁₆ inch) plain nozzle. Set aside and keep warm.

This can be made up to 1 day in advance and stored in an airtight container in the fridge. Reheat before serving.

PEA CRUMBS

150 ml (5 fl oz) warm pea purée
15 g (½ oz) maltodextrin
40 g (1½ oz) ground almonds (almond meal)
15 g (½ oz) black sesame seeds

Combine the purée and maltodextrin well. Spread evenly over a non-stick baking mat to 3 mm (⅛ inch) thick and place on a baking tray. Dry in a dehydrator at 80ºC (176ºF) for 1 hour. Alternatively, place in the oven on the lowest temperature and leave until completely dry. Remove and allow to cool. Scrape into a food processor, add the ground almonds and pulse until fine crumbs form. Transfer to a bowl and stir in the sesame seeds. Set aside.

This can be made up to 1 day in advance and stored in an airtight container in the fridge.

PEA GEL

1½ sheets gelatine, titanium strength
150 ml (5 fl oz) pea purée

Place the gelatine in cold water for 5 minutes or until softened. Place the pea purée in a small saucepan over medium heat. Squeeze out the excess water from the gelatine and add the gelatine to the pan, stirring until dissolved. Pour into a container and refrigerate for 1 hour or until set. This can be made up to 1 day in advance.

PEA FONDANT ASSEMBLY

Slice the pea gel into 1.5 cm (⅝ inch) cubes. Lay plastic wrap over a small dariole mould and depress the centre slightly. Pipe 10 g (⅓ oz) of the black sesame purée onto the plastic wrap and place a cube of pea gel on top. Pipe another 10 g of black sesame purée on top, making sure the pea gel is completely covered and there are no air pockets. Take all 4 corners of the plastic wrap, twist together to form a tight ball and tie tightly to secure. Repeat to make 8 balls.

These can be made 1 day in advance and refrigerated. When ready to serve, heat a saucepan of water to 90ºC (194ºF) and poach the balls for 3 minutes. Scoop out and remove the plastic wrap. Serve immediately.

MINT OIL

1 bunch (50 g/1¾ oz) mint, leaves picked
100 ml (3½ fl oz) vegetable oil

Blanch the mint in boiling water for 1 minute. Drain and refresh in iced water. Drain again and squeeze out the excess water. Place the leaves in an upright blender with the oil and blend until smooth. Pass through a fine sieve. Set aside. This recipe makes more than you will need.

GOAT'S CURD DRESSING

120 g (4¼ oz) goat's curd
40 ml (1¼ fl oz) extra virgin olive oil
freshly ground white pepper
2 teaspoons lemon juice

Place the goat's curd and oil in an upright blender and blend until smooth. Season with white pepper and lemon juice. Transfer half of the dressing to a piping bag fitted with a 2 mm (¹⁄₁₆ inch) plain nozzle. Set aside.

SNOW PEAS AND PEAS

50 g (1¾ oz) snow peas (mangetout), trimmed
½ quantity goat's curd dressing,
   plus 20 g (⅔ oz) extra
mint oil, to taste
lemon juice, to taste
sea salt flakes
50 g (1¾ oz) podded green peas
   (about 125 g/4½ oz unpodded)

Thinly slice the snow peas lengthways, avoiding the section that contains the peas — discard this section. Place the snow peas in a bowl, add the goat's curd dressing, dress with a little of the mint oil and lemon juice and season with salt. Mix to coat well. Divide into 6 equal bundles with the ends neatly lined up. Trim the ends, then cut each bundle into 2 cm (¾ inch) sections. Set aside.

Bring 500 ml (17 fl oz/2 cups) water to the boil. Blanch the peas for 1 minute. Drain and refresh in iced water. Drain again, then remove the skins from the peas. Thinly slice the peas, place in a bowl, add the extra goat's curd dressing, dress with a little of the mint oil and lemon juice and season with salt. Set aside.

PRESENTATION

red garnet shoots , for garnish

Place 3 piles of pea crumbs onto each of 6 plates. Arrange 2 snow pea stacks at opposite ends of the plate. Arrange 2 piles of peeled peas on opposite ends of each plate. Pipe 3 small dots of the goat's curd dressing onto each plate. Pipe 3 small dots of pea purée onto each plate. Place a pea fondant on top of each pea crumb pile and rest a piece of black sesame glass on top. Garnish with the red garnet shoots. Serves 6.

JERUSALEM ARTICHOKE CUSTARD WITH SOY AND BORLOTTI BEANS

JERUSALEM ARTICHOKE CUSTARD

500 g (1 lb 2 oz) Jerusalem artichokes, peeled
50 g (1¾ oz) unsalted butter
sea salt and freshly ground white pepper
4 eggs
2 g (⅟₁₆ oz) gellan gum

Slice the artichokes into 1 cm (½ inch) thick pieces. Place in a saucepan over medium heat with the butter and 400 ml (14 fl oz) water. Season and cook for 30 minutes or until softened and the water is evaporated. Drain and place in a blender with the eggs and gellan. Blend until smooth. Pass through a sieve. Return to the pan, place over medium heat and cook, stirring continuously, until the purée reaches 85°C (185°F). Transfer to a metal bowl and chill over ice to firm up. Place in a piping bag fitted with a 1.5 cm (⅝ inch) plain nozzle. This can be made 1 day in advance and refrigerated. Bring to room temperature before serving.

BRIK PASTRY

20 g (⅔ oz) clarified butter, melted
2 sheets brik pastry (see Note)

Preheat oven to 170°C (325°F/Gas 3). Brush the butter over the pastry. Cut the pastry into 18 small triangles, place on a baking tray lined with baking paper, cover with more paper, then place another tray on top to weight down and keep it flat. Bake for 7 minutes or until crisp. Cool.

NOTE Brik pastry is thin Tunisian pastry similar to spring roll wrappers. Buy it from gourmet food stores.

SOY AND BORLOTTI BEANS

6 baby beetroot, scrubbed and trimmed
vegetable oil, for deep-frying
6 chestnuts
3 heads new season (green) garlic, halved
2 radishes, trimmed and quartered
300 ml (10½ fl oz) olive oil
200 g (7 oz) podded fresh borlotti beans
    (about 500 g/1 lb 2 oz unpodded)
sea salt flakes and freshly ground black pepper
50 g (1¾ oz) butter
200 g (7 oz) podded soy (edamame) beans

Preheat the oven to 170°C (325°F/Gas 3). Wrap the beetroot in foil and bake for 30 minutes or until tender. When cool enough to handle, peel and halve.

Heat the vegetable oil in a small deep saucepan or deep-fryer to 170°C (325°F). Using a small sharp knife, score a cross at the tips of the chestnuts. Deep-fry for 2 minutes, then remove using tongs and drain well on paper towel. Cool slightly, then peel the shells and papery skins.

Place the chestnuts, garlic, radish and olive oil in a saucepan over low heat and cook. Remove the radish after 5 minutes and set aside. Continue to cook the chestnuts and garlic for another 15 minutes or until softened. The chestnuts may need to be removed earlier, if they have softened. Drain and set aside.

Place the borlotti beans in a small saucepan, cover with water, add 2 g (⅟₁₆ oz) salt and cook over medium heat for 12 minutes or until tender. Drain and set aside.

Heat the butter and 30 ml (1 fl oz) water in a frying pan over medium heat. Add the radish, chestnuts, garlic, beetroot and soy beans and cook for 1 minute or until warmed through. Season with salt and pepper and serve.

MUSTARD DRESSING

40 g (1½ oz) Dijon mustard
20 ml (⅔ fl oz) sherry vinegar
40 ml (1½ fl oz) vegetable oil
20 ml (⅔ fl oz) extra virgin olive oil

Whisk the mustard and vinegar in a bowl until combined. While whisking, gradually pour in the oils, whisking until emulsified. Place in a sauce bottle and set aside.

PRESENTATION

mustard cress shoots and nasturtium leaves

Pipe the custard onto 6 plates. Arrange the vegetables around the custard and dot around the dressing. Insert the brik triangles into the custard and garnish. Serves 6.

SLOW-COOKED PORK BELLY WITH APPLE, TONKA BEAN AND RED MISO

PORK BUBBLE

500 g (1 lb 2 oz) piece of pork skin
500 ml (17 fl oz/2 cups) vegetable oil

Place the skin and 2 litres (70 fl oz) water in a saucepan and bring to the boil. Reduce heat to low and simmer for 4 hours or until the skin is soft, topping up with water to keep the skin covered, if necessary. Allow to cool in the liquid. Drain and place flat on a tray and refrigerate overnight.

Using a sharp knife, trim the fat from the skin, being careful to keep the skin intact. Place on a baking tray lined with baking paper. Dry in a dehydrator at 60°C (140°F) for 6 hours. Alternatively, place in the oven on the lowest temperature and leave until completely dry.

When ready to serve, snap the skin into about 4 cm (1½ inch) squares. Heat the oil in a deep-fryer or deep saucepan to 180°C (350°F). Deep-fry the pork skin for 1 minute, then remove and drain on paper towel. Cut into thin strips.

APPLE AND TONKA BEAN JELLY

5 green apples, peeled
2 teaspoons lemon juice
1 tonka bean, finely grated using a microplane grater
2 g (¹⁄₁₆ oz) xanthan gum
1 g (¹⁄₃₂ oz) kappa
1 g (¹⁄₃₂ oz) iota

Line the base and sides of a 30 x 25 cm (12 x 10 inch) tray with freezer film. Quarter the apples and remove the cores. Place in a saucepan, cover with water, add the lemon juice and bring to the boil. Reduce the heat to low and simmer for 15 minutes or until very soft. Strain, discarding solids. Return the liquid to the pan, place over medium heat and cook until reduced to 250 ml (9 fl oz/ 1 cup). Add the tonka bean, xanthan gum, kappa and iota and bring to the boil for 1 minute. Spread evenly over the lined tray and refrigerate for 1 hour or until set.

This can be made up to 1 day in advance. When ready to serve, cut the jelly into six 15 x 3 cm (6 x 1¼ inch) strips. Set aside.

RED MISO OIL

125 ml (4 fl oz/½ cup) vegetable oil
15 g (½ oz) red miso
5 g (¹⁄₆ oz) sweet paprika

Place all the ingredients in an upright blender and blend until well combined. Pass through a fine sieve. Set aside.

This can be made 1 day in advance and stored in an airtight container in the fridge.

EMULSIFIED RED MISO OIL

¼ sheet gelatine, titanium strength
0.5 g pectin
0.15 g agar agar
125 ml (4 fl oz/½ cup) red miso oil
sea salt flakes

Soak the gelatine in a bowl of water for 5 minutes or until softened. Place the pectin, agar agar and 25 ml (⁴⁄₅ fl oz) water in a small saucepan and bring to the boil. Squeeze out the excess water from the gelatine and add the gelatine to the pan, stirring until dissolved. Cool slightly. While blending, using a stick blender, gradually add the miso oil, blending until emulsified. Season with salt. Place in a piping bag fitted with a 2 mm (¹⁄₁₆ inch) plain nozzle. Set aside.

This can be made 1 day in advance and stored in an airtight container in the fridge.

PORK BELLY

1 litre (35 fl oz/4 cups) milk
800 g (1 lb 12 oz) boneless pork belly, skin on
1 fresh bay leaf
3 whole allspice
10 black peppercorns
20 ml (⅔ fl oz) olive oil

Preheat the oven to 160ºC (315ºF/Gas 2–3). Place the milk, pork belly, bay leaf and spices in an ovenproof saucepan and bring to the boil. Cover with a cartouche, then a lid, and bake for 2½ hours or until tender. Allow to cool. Remove the pork and discard the cooking liquid. Remove the pork skin and discard. Cut the meat into 6 equal portions.

When ready to serve, heat the oil in a frying pan over high heat and sear the pork all over. Carve each portion into 4 equal pieces.

MISO RICE BALLS

100 g (3½ oz/½ cup) long-grain rice
1½ teaspoons mirin
15 g (½ oz) red miso
finely grated zest of ½ lime
vegetable oil, for deep-frying

Place the rice and 200 ml (7 fl oz) water in a saucepan over medium heat. Cover and cook for 15 minutes or until the water is absorbed and the rice is very soft. Remove from the heat and add the mirin, red miso and lime zest. Push through a food mill (mouli).

Shape teaspoons of the mixture into small balls. You will need 24 balls. Heat the oil in a large deep saucepan or deep-fryer to 170ºC (325ºF). Deep-fry the balls for 2 minutes or until crisp all over. Remove using tongs and drain well on paper towel. Serve immediately.

GREEN OLIVE PURÉE

200 g (7 oz) Sicilian green olives, pitted
30 ml (1 fl oz) extra virgin olive oil

Place the olives in a saucepan, cover with water and bring to the boil, then drain. Transfer to an upright blender, add the oil and blend until smooth. Pass through a fine sieve. Set aside.

APPLE AND GREEN OLIVE SALSA

1 green apple, peeled, halved and core removed
6 Sicilian green olives, pitted
1 sprig dill, leaves picked
2 sprigs flat-leaf (Italian) parsley, leaves picked
2 teaspoons lemon juice
20 ml (⅔ fl oz) extra virgin olive oil
sea salt flakes

Finely dice the apple. Dice the olives into 2 mm (1/16 inch) cubes. Chop the dill and parsley leaves and combine with the apple and olive. Dress with the lemon juice and oil and season with salt. Set aside.

PRESENTATION

Pipe dots of the purée diagonally across 6 plates. Place small piles of the salsa alternating with the purée. Place 2 pieces of pork alongide the salsa, leaving a space in between. Lay the jelly over the 2 pieces of pork. Take 2 more pieces of pork and place alternately between the first 2 — this will create a weave, one piece over the jelly and the next piece under it. Arrange 4 miso rice balls around the pork. Pipe small dots of emulsified miso oil around the plate and garnish with the pork bubble. Serves 6.

CITRUS-GLAZED MACKEREL WITH TARTINE OF ALMOND AND PARMESAN AND SOFT HERB SALAD

ALMOND AND PARMESAN

50 g (1¾ oz) sourdough bread, crusts removed
100 g (3½ oz/1 cup) finely grated parmesan
50 g (1¾ oz/⅓ cup) blanched almonds, toasted
sea salt flakes

Preheat the oven to 160°C (315°F/Gas 2–3). Place the bread on a baking tray and bake for 10 minutes or until very crisp. Using a sharp knife, thinly slice the bread so it shatters. Set aside.

Sprinkle the parmesan in an even layer over a baking tray lined with baking paper and bake for 7 minutes or until melted and bubbling. Remove and cool on the tray.

Thinly slice the toasted almonds. Break the parmesan into small pieces, combine with the almonds and breadcrumbs in a bowl and season with salt. Set aside.

SOFT HERB SALAD

½ store-bought preserved lemon
1 sprig flat-leaf (Italian) parsley, leaves picked
1 sprig dill, leaves picked
10 g (⅓ oz) rocket shoots
3 chives, cut into batons
1 eschalot (French shallot), finely diced
2 teaspoons lemon juice
3 teaspoons extra virgin olive oil
sea salt flakes

Remove and finely dice the peel of the preserved lemon, discarding the pulp. Combine the herbs, preserved lemon and eschalot in a bowl, dress with the lemon juice and oil and season with the salt. Set aside.

CITRUS-GLAZED MACKEREL

2 lemons
60 g (2 oz) honey
60 ml (2 fl oz/¼ cup) soy sauce
25 ml (⅘ fl oz) sherry vinegar
6 slimy mackerel fillets, skin on and pin-boned
sea salt flakes
20 ml (⅔ oz) olive oil

Using a microplane grater, finely grate half the zest of one lemon, then juice both lemons. Place the honey and soy sauce in a small saucepan and bring to the boil. Add the vinegar, lemon zest and 100 ml (3½ fl oz) lemon juice and cook for 1 minute. Set aside.

Trim the mackerel so each fillet is a neat rectangle, then season with salt. Heat a frying pan over high heat. Add the oil, then the mackerel, skin-side down. Sear for 1–2 minutes, then turn and immediately remove from the pan. The mackerel should still be a little rare in the middle. Brush a little of the citrus glaze over the mackerel and serve immediately.

PRESENTATION

Place the almond and parmesan on 6 plates and place the mackerel on top. Arrange the herb salad over the mackerel and sauce the dish with the remaining citrus glaze. Serves 6.

CHESTNUT SOUP, FOIE GRAS, PUFFED WHEAT, PINE NUTS AND PICKLED RAISINS

PUFFED WHEAT, PINE NUTS AND PICKLED RAISINS

100 g (3½ oz/heaped ½ cup) coarse cracked wheat (burghul)
510 ml (17⅓ fl oz) vegetable oil
100 g (3½ oz/⅔ cup) pine nuts
100 ml (3½ fl oz) rice vinegar
75 ml (2⅔ fl oz) maple syrup
50 g (1¾ oz/heaped ⅓ cup) raisins

Place the wheat in a small saucepan and cover with water. Bring to the boil, then reduce the heat to low and simmer for 20 minutes or until softened. Strain, then spread over a baking tray lined with baking paper. Dry in a dehydrator at 60°C (140°F) for 2 hours. Alternatively, place in the oven on the lowest temperature and leave until completely dry.

Heat 500 ml (17 fl oz/2 cups) oil to 200°C (400°F) in a deep saucepan or deep-fryer. Place the wheat in a metal sieve and deep-fry for 30 seconds or until puffed up. Remove and drain on paper towel. Allow to cool.

Heat the remaining oil in a small non-stick frying pan over medium heat. Add the pine nuts and cook, tossing regularly, until golden. Drain on paper towel and allow to cool.

Bring the vinegar and maple syrup to the boil. Pour over the raisins and allow to cool.

When ready to serve, strain the raisins, discarding the liquid, and quarter each widthways. Combine with the puffed wheat and and pine nuts.

FOIE GRAS PARFAIT

1 length 1 cm (½ inch) diameter PVC piping
1 sheet acetate
1 garlic clove, thinly sliced
3 teaspoons milk
200 g (7 oz) pasteurised foie gras
110 g (3¾ oz) unsalted butter, softened
2 g (¹⁄₁₆ oz) sea salt flakes

Cut the PVC piping into six 10 cm (4 inch) long pieces. Cut the acetate into six 12 x 5 cm (4½ x 2 inch) rectangles. Roll each piece widthways, then place each roll inside a piece of PVC pipe. Make sure one end of the acetate sits flush with the pipe and the other end protrudes. Place plastic wrap over the flush end and secure with tape. Stand, covered-end down, on a tray.

Heat the garlic and milk in a small saucepan over low heat for 2 minutes.

Place the foie gras, butter and salt in an upright blender and blend until smooth. Add the warm milk mixture and blend again until smooth, then pass through a fine sieve. Pour into the moulds filling only to the top of the pipe and refrigerate for 2 hours or until set.

CHESTNUT SOUP

vegetable oil, for deep-frying
250 g (9 oz) chestnuts (see Note)
1 small onion, chopped
2 garlic cloves, chopped
30 ml (1 fl oz) olive oil
1 fresh bay leaf
4 sprigs thyme

Heat the vegetable oil in a small deep saucepan or deep-fryer to 170°C (325°F). Using a small sharp knife, score a cross at the tips of the chestnuts. Deep-fry for 2 minutes, then remove using tongs and drain well on paper towel. Cool slightly, but while still warm, peel off the shells and papery skin.

Place the onion, garlic and olive oil in a small saucepan over medium heat. Cook, stirring occasionally, for about 5 minutes or until softened. Tie the bay leaf and thyme together with kitchen string and add to the pan. Add the chestnuts and cook for 3 minutes. Cover with water and bring to the boil. Reduce the heat to low and simmer for 20 minutes or until very tender. Discard the bay leaf and thyme. Transfer the mixture to an upright blender and blend until smooth. Pass through a fine sieve. Transfer to a cream canister and charge twice. Set aside in a warm place.

NOTE If using frozen chestnuts, place them in a roasting tray and toss in 50 ml (1¾ fl oz) vegetable oil. Roast in a preheated 180°C (350°F) oven for 30 minutes or until golden. Cool slightly, peel and use as above.

PRESENTATION

30 g (1 oz) dehydrated capers (see Masterclass, page 20)
6 rosemary flowers

Place the puffed wheat, pine nuts and pickled raisins to one side of 6 bowls. Take the parfaits out of the fridge. To remove the parfaits, remove the plastic wrap and tape, then use the protruding acetate to carefully pull them out of the moulds — the acetate will naturally uncurl from around the parfaits. Use the acetate to transfer the parfaits to lie on top of the puffed wheat. Garnish with the dehydrated capers and flowers. Fill the other half of the bowls with the chestnut soup. Serves 6.

RED MULLET WITH WHITE BEAN AND JAMÓN 'GNOCCHI' AND SAFFRON

DEHYDRATED WAKAME

50 g (1½ oz) fresh wakame (see Note)
2 teaspoons olive oil

Rub the wakame with the oil and spread out flat on a baking tray lined with baking paper. Dry in a dehydrator at 60°C (140°F) for 4 hours. Alternatively, place in the oven on the lowest temperature and leave until completely dry and crisp.

This can be made 1 day in advance and stored in an airtight container in a dry place.

NOTE If fresh wakame isn't available, you can substitute dried wakame, available from Japanese grocers. You will need to rehydrate it in water first, then stretch it out flat before dehydrating.

JAMÓN STOCK

150 g (5½ oz) jamón, cut into large dice
1 stalk celery, chopped
1 carrot, chopped
1 onion, chopped
1 head garlic, halved widthways
1 fresh bay leaf
2 sprigs thyme

Place all the ingredients in a saucepan. Add 1.2 litres (42 fl oz) water and bring to the boil, then reduce the heat to 85°C (185°F) and simmer for 2 hours, keeping the stock at 85°C and skimming the scum from the surface regularly. Strain, discarding the solids.

SAFFRON SAUCE

½ quantity jamón stock
0.25 g saffron (about 50 threads)

Place the stock and saffron in a saucepan and heat to 85°C (185°F). Simmer for 20 minutes, keeping the stock at 85°C, to infuse. Strain through a fine sieve. Set aside and keep warm.

WHITE BEAN AND JAMÓN 'GNOCCHI'

6 g (⅕) calcium chloride
½ quantity jamón stock
200 g (7 oz) dried white beans, soaked overnight,
    drained
5 g (⅙ oz) sodium alginate
sea salt flakes

Combine the calcium chloride with 500 ml (17 fl oz/2 cups) water. Set calcium bath aside.

Place the stock and beans in a saucepan and bring to the boil, then simmer for 1 hour or until the beans are tender. Drain, then transfer the beans to an upright blender and blend until smooth. Add the alginate and season with salt. Pass through a fine sieve.

Transfer to a piping bag fitted with a plain 1.5 cm (⅝ inch) nozzle. Pipe 12 cm (4½ inch) lengths into the calcium bath. Leave in the bath for 3 minutes or until a skin forms. Use kitchen scissors to cut into 3 cm (1¼ inch) lengths. Scoop out using a slotted spoon, then rinse in a clean water bath. Scoop out again and drain on paper towel.

These can be made up to 1 hour in advance. When ready to serve, place the 'gnocchi' in a steamer over simmering water and gently reheat.

RED MULLET

12 red mullet fillets, skin on and pin-boned
sea salt flakes
2 teaspoons olive oil

Season the mullet with salt. Heat the oil in a non-stick frying pan over high heat. Cook the mullet, skin-side down, for 1 minute. Turn the fish, then remove from the pan. Set aside and keep warm.

BABY ABALONE

½ brown onion, chopped
1 carrot, chopped
1 stalk celery, chopped
2 garlic cloves
3 fresh bay leaves
5 sprigs thyme
20 black peppercorns
300 ml (10½ fl oz) white wine
50 ml (1¾ fl oz) white wine vinegar
peel of 1 lemon, white pith removed
2 baby abalone
sea salt flakes

Place the vegetables, garlic, herbs, peppercorns, wine, vinegar, lemon peel and 1.5 litres (52 fl oz) water in a large saucepan and bring to the boil. Add the abalone, return to the boil, then reduce the heat to low and simmer for 15 minutes. Remove the abalone from their shells and cut into 2 mm (¹⁄₁₆ inch) thick slices. Serve immediately.

PRESENTATION

2 g (¹⁄₁₆ oz) powdered wakame (see Note)

Divide the 'gnocchi' between 6 plates and sprinkle over the powdered wakame. Scatter around the abalone, place 2 mullet fillets on opposite sides of the plate, garnish with the dehydrated wakame and pour over the saffron sauce. Serves 6.

NOTE Powdered wakame is available from Japanese grocers.

'ROASTED' QUAIL WITH SILVERBEET, QUINOA, FETA AND BARBERRY

FETA BALLS

100 g (3½ oz) feta
3 g (⅒ oz) methylcellulose
2 sheets gelatine, titanium strength
0.25 g xanthan gum
80 g (2¾ oz) silverbeet (Swiss chard) leaves, trimmed
80 g (2¾ oz) quinoa (see Note)
2 garlic cloves, finely diced
¼ bunch (10 g/⅓ oz) mint, leaves picked and finely chopped
½ store-bought preserved lemon, peel only, finely diced

Place the feta and 125 ml (4 fl oz/½ cup) water in an upright blender and blend until smooth. Add the methylcellulose. Soak the gelatine in cold water for 5 minutes or until softened. Squeeze out the excess water, then melt in a double boiler over simmering water. Add to the feta mixture and combine. Spread over a large tray lined with freezer film to 1 mm (1/32 inch thick). Place in the freezer and chill until 1–4°C (34–39°F), then cut into twelve 4 cm (1½ inch) squares. Set aside. Bring a saucepan of water to the boil. Blanch the silverbeet for 1 minute. Drain, refresh in iced water, drain again and squeeze out the excess water. Chop finely and set aside. Place the quinoa in a small saucepan and cover with water. Cook over medium heat for 20 minutes or until softened. Strain and add to the silverbeet with the garlic, mint and preserved lemon and stir to combine.

Place a piece of feta on a 30 cm (12 inch) square piece of plastic wrap. Top the feta with 15 g (½ oz) of the silverbeet mixture. Take all 4 corners of the plastic wrap and twist together to form a tight ball and tie off to secure. Repeat to make 12 balls. These can be made 1 day in advance and refrigerated. When ready to serve, heat a saucepan of water to 80°C (176°F) and poach the balls for 4 minutes. Scoop out and remove the plastic. Set aside.

NOTE Quinoa is a small seed, available from health food stores.

BARBERRY SAUCE

80 g (2¾ oz) dried barberries (see Note)
20 ml (⅔ fl oz) olive oil
10 g (⅓ oz) caster (superfine) sugar
0.25 g xanthan gum
sea salt flakes

Soak the barberries in cold water for 1 hour. Drain. Place in an upright blender. Add 160 ml (5¼ fl oz) water, the oil, sugar and xanthan gum and blend until smooth. Pass through a fine sieve. Season with salt. Set aside.

NOTE Dried barberries are available from health food stores and Middle Eastern grocers.

GLAZE

40 g (1½ oz) rock sugar
40 ml (1¼ fl oz) oyster sauce
60 ml (2 fl oz/¼ cup) soy sauce

Place all the ingredients in a small saucepan over medium heat, stirring until the sugar is dissolved. Set aside and allow to cool.

This can be made 1 day in advance and stored in an airtight container in the fridge.

'ROASTED' QUAIL

6 quails, butterflied
35 g (1¼ oz) egg white (about 1 egg)
125 ml (4 fl oz/½ cup) pouring (single) cream
sea salt flakes
1 quantity glaze
vegetable oil, for deep-frying

Working with one quail at a time, lay one, skin-side up, on a work surface with the legs closest to you. Take the inside of the top of a leg and gently pull towards you to remove it, taking care to leave the leg skin attached to the body. Repeat with the other leg. Set aside.

Remove the bones from the underside of the breasts but do not separate the pair of fillets. Refrigerate until required.

Using a sharp knife, remove the leg meat from the bones. Roughly chop and place in a food processor with the egg white and cream. Season with salt and process until smooth. Pass through a drum sieve (tamis). Transfer to a piping bag fitted with a 1 cm (½ inch) plain nozzle and refrigerate until chilled.

Working with one pair of quail breasts at a time, place the breasts, skin-side down, on a work surface. Pipe a 1 cm (½ inch) thick line of purée widthways across the breasts. Using the edge of the skin as a guide, roll the breasts up around the filling to form a cylinder. Lay a piece of plastic wrap on a work surface and brush all over with the glaze. Roll the plastic wrap tightly around the quail and tie off the ends to secure.

Heat a saucepan of water to 60°C (140°F). Poach the quail cylinders for 30 minutes. Scoop out and remove the plastic wrap.

Heat the oil in a large deep saucepan or deep-fryer to 180°C (350°F). Deep-fry the quail for 1 minute or until crisp all over. Remove using tongs and drain on paper towel. Slice widthways into 3 equal pieces. Serve immediately.

PRESENTATION

mint shoots, for garnish
sea salt flakes
smoked paprika, for sprinkling

Spread some barberry sauce onto 6 plates. Arrange 3 pieces of quail around the plate. Arrange 2 feta balls between the quail pieces. Sprinkle the quail with the salt and the balls with smoked paprika. Garnish with the mint shoots. Serves 6.

POACHED BACALAO WITH SMOKED POTATO MOUSSE, MUSSELS AND PIPIS

SMOKED POTATO MOUSSE

2 large desiree potatoes, unpeeled
25 ml (⅘ fl oz) olive oil
sea salt flakes
30 g (1 oz) smoking chips
400 ml (14 fl oz) milk
1 g (⅟₃₂ oz) xanthan gum

Preheat the oven to 160°C (315°F/Gas 2–3). Drizzle the potatoes with the oil and season with salt, then wrap each in foil. Place on a baking tray and bake for 40 minutes or until cooked through. Remove from the oven and allow to cool. Remove the skin and quarter the flesh.

Place the smoking chips in the bottom half of a steamer and the potato in the top half. Place over high heat and once smoke appears, remove from the heat. Stand for 8 minutes or until the smoke has evaporated. Remove the potato, place in a saucepan, cover with the milk and bring to the boil. Set aside for 1 hour to infuse. Transfer the potato and milk to a blender, add the xanthan gum and blend until smooth. Pass through a sieve. Transfer to a cream canister and charge twice. Refrigerate until required.

This can be made 1 day in advance. When ready to serve, heat the mixture by placing the canister in hot water.

BACALAO

6 x 60 g (2¼ oz) pieces of bacalao (see Note)
120 ml (4 fl oz) extra virgin olive oil
3 teaspoons lemon juice

Cover the bacalao with water and leave to soak for 24 hours, draining and covering with fresh water every 8 hours. Drain and pat dry with paper towel. Remove any scales from the skin. Place each piece in a vacuum-seal or zip-lock bag and add 20 ml (⅔ fl oz) oil. Heat a saucepan of water to 68°C (154°F). Follow the Masterclass on sous-vide cooking (see page 16) and cook the fish for 6 minutes. Remove from the water and keep warm. When ready to serve, remove from the bags and drizzle with the lemon juice.

NOTE Bacalao is a traditional Spanish and Portuguese dish, commonly called salted cod. There are many types. I like the one from the Basque country, and I prefer to use the loin as it has less bones and a better texture. Bacalao is available from Spanish, Portuguese and Italian grocers.

MUSSELS AND PIPIS

100 ml (3½ fl oz) white wine
2 fresh bay leaves
2 sprigs thyme
6 black peppercorns
12 mussels, scrubbed and debearded
18 pipis, purged and drained

Place half of each of the wine, bay leaf, thyme and peppercorns in a small saucepan and bring to the boil. Add the mussels and cover with a glass lid. As the mussels open, remove from the pan. Discard the cooking liquid. Repeat with the pipis and remaining ingredients. Remove the mussels and pipis from their shells and keep warm.

NEW SEASON GARLIC EMULSION

⅓ bunch (40 g/1½ oz) flat-leaf (Italian) parsley, leaves picked
2 heads new season (green) garlic, bulbs only
100 ml (3½ fl oz) vegetable oil
1 quantity mussels and pipis
1 bunch (20 g/¾ oz) chives, finely chopped

Place the parsley and garlic in an upright blender and blend until finely chopped. With the motor running, gradually add the oil and blend until smooth. Pass through a fine sieve. Place the mussels and pipis in a bowl and dress with the garlic emulsion and chives. Serve immediately.

PRESENTATION

20 g (⅔ oz) samphire
borage flowers, for garnish

Place the bacalao to one side of 6 plates. Arrange 3 pipis and 2 mussels on the other side and pipe dots of the mousse between. Arrange the samphire on top of the shellfish and garnish with the flowers. Serves 6.

CARAMELISED PORK CHEEK WITH BEETROOT AND SALMON 'RAVIOLI'

BEETROOT GEL

2 large beetroot (about 500 g/1 lb 2 oz in total)
500 ml (17 fl oz/2 cups) white chicken stock (see page 22)
2 teaspoons balsamic vinegar
3 garlic cloves
6 g (⅕ oz) coriander seed
2 g (¹⁄₁₆ oz) cumin seeds
0.5 g whole allspice
15 black peppercorns
1 cinnamon stick
1 star anise
1 fresh bay leaf
10 g (⅓ oz/½ bunch) thyme
sea salt flakes
5 g (⅙ oz) agar agar

Peel and thinly slice the beetroot, place in a large saucepan, add the stock, vinegar, garlic, spices, herbs and 500 ml (17 fl oz/2 cups) water and bring to the boil. Reduce the heat to low and simmer for 2 hours. Strain, discarding the solids. Return the liquid to the pan and simmer until reduced to 500 ml (17 fl oz/2 cups). Season with salt. Add the agar agar and cook, stirring continuously, until dissolved. Transfer to a metal bowl and chill over ice until set. Transfer the gel to an upright blender and blend until smooth. Pass through a fine sieve and set aside.

This can be made 1 day in advance and stored in an airtight container in the fridge.

PORK CHEEK

300 ml (10½ fl oz) white chicken stock (see page 22)
300 ml (10½ fl oz) milk
4 fresh bay leaves
½ bunch (10 g/⅓ oz) thyme, leaves picked
20 g (⅔ oz) sea salt flakes
3 pork cheeks (about 900 g/2 lb in total)
20 ml (⅔ fl oz) vegetable oil

Preheat the oven to 150°C (300°F/Gas 2). Place the stock, milk, bay leaves, thyme and salt in an ovenproof saucepan and bring to the boil. Add the pork cheeks, cover and bake for 2½ hours or until tender. Allow to cool completely in the liquid. Remove the cheeks from the liquid and discard the liquid. Trim the excess fat from the cheeks, then halve each lengthways to form 2 rectangles. Heat the oil in a frying pan and sear the pork cheeks all over. Serve immediately.

BEETROOT AND SALMON 'RAVIOLI'

2 large beetroot (about 500 g/1 lb 2 oz in total), scrubbed and trimmed
50 ml (1¾ fl oz) Forum chardonnay vinegar
25 ml (⅘ fl oz) rice vinegar
5 g (⅙ oz) coriander seeds
2 fresh bay leaves
40 g (1½ oz) caster (superfine) sugar
10 g (⅓ oz) sea salt flakes
5 g (⅙ oz) black peppercorns
200 g (7 oz) smoked salmon (see Masterclass, page 19) (see Note)
40 g (1½ oz) crème fraîche
10 g (⅓ oz) fresh horseradish, peeled and finely grated
2 sprigs (10 g/⅓ oz) dill, leaves picked and chopped

Peel and, using a mandolin, thinly slice the beetroot into 1 mm (¹⁄₃₂ inch) thick slices. Select the best 24 slices and place in a heatproof bowl. Place the vinegars, coriander seeds, bay leaves, sugar, salt, peppercorns and 75 ml (2⅔ fl oz) water in a saucepan and bring to the boil. Pour over the beetroot, cover with plastic wrap and refrigerate for 3 hours to pickle.

Dice the smoked salmon into 5 mm (¼ inch) cubes and combine with the crème fraîche, horseradish and dill.

Drain the beetroot, discarding the liquid. Place half of the slices on a work surface and place a teaspoon of the salmon mixture in the centre of each slice. Top with the remaining slices. Using the blunt edge of a 3 cm (1¼ inch) round cutter, make an indent around the filling without cutting all the way through. Using a 5 cm (2 inch) round cutter, cut out rounds from the beetroot slices and discard the trimmings. Set aside.

These can be made 1 day in advance and stored in an airtight container in the fridge.

NOTE You can substitute with store-bought smoked salmon.

TROUT ROE VINAIGRETTE

100 ml (3½ fl oz) veal jus (see page 24)
75 ml (2⅔ fl oz) extra virgin olive oil
30 g (1 oz) trout roe
2 teaspoons lemon juice
½ bunch (10 g/⅓ oz) chives, finely chopped

Gently combine all the ingredients in a bowl.

PRESENTATION

Place a piece of pork cheek in the centre of 6 plates. Using 2 teaspoons, place a quenelle of beetroot gel on one side of the pork cheek. Arrange a raviolo on either side of the pork. Dress with the vinaigrette. Serves 6.

MAINS

When it comes to the main course, my approach is quite simple, so not surprisingly, these recipes are the easiest dishes to execute. Mains are all about showcasing the great produce that is available in Australia. In most cases, I try to do as little to a particular piece of meat or seafood as possible. I make the protein the centrepiece and complement it with interesting, sometimes unusual, garnishes.

'ROASTED' SPATCHCOCK WITH SWEETCORN POLENTA, PISTACHIO AND ASPARAGUS

GLAZE

40 g (1½ oz) rock sugar
60 ml (2 fl oz/¼ cup) soy sauce
40 ml (1¼ fl oz) oyster sauce

Place the ingredients in a small saucepan over medium heat, stirring until the sugar is dissolved. Cool and set aside.

'ROASTED' SPATCHCOCK

6 spatchcocks (baby chickens), butterflied
sea salt and freshly ground black pepper
1 head garlic, cloves separated and sliced
½ bunch (10 g/⅓ oz) thyme
2 fresh bay leaves
olive oil, to cover
40 g (1½ oz) Dijon mustard
vegetable oil, for deep-frying
1 quantity glaze
1 egg, lightly beaten
100 g (3½ oz/⅔ cup) fine polenta

Working with one spatchcock at a time, lay one, skin-side up, on a work surface with the legs closest to you. Take the inside of the top of a leg and gently pull towards you to remove it, taking care to leave the leg skin attached to the body. Repeat with the other leg. Set aside.

Remove the bones from the underside of the breasts but do not separate the pair of fillets. Refrigerate until needed.

Using a sharp knife, remove the leg meat from the bones. Scatter over 6 g (⅕ oz) salt, garlic, thyme and bay leaves and refrigerate for 1 hour.

Preheat the oven to 150°C (300°F/Gas 2). Rinse the salt off the spatchcock legs and pat dry with paper towel. Place in a roasting tray, cover with the olive oil and bake for 1 hour. Remove from the oven and allow to cool in the oil. Pick the meat off the bones. Season with mustard, salt and pepper. Press the meat into a 15 x 10 cm (6 x 4 inch) plastic container and refrigerate until chilled.

Meanwhile, working with a pair of spatchcock breasts and season with salt and pepper. Form the breast into a ball and tie off using kitchen string. Place a square of plastic wrap on a work surface, brush with the glaze and place the ball in the centre. Take all 4 corners of the plastic wrap and twist together to form a tight ball. Tie off tightly to secure. Heat a saucepan of water to 68°C (154°F). Poach the balls for 30 minutes. Scoop out and remove the plastic wrap. Set aside.

When ready to serve, heat the vegetable oil in a large deep saucepan or deep-fryer to 170°C (325°F). Turn the leg meat out onto a chopping board and cut into 6 equal rectangles. Dip in the beaten egg, then roll in the polenta to coat well and deep-fry for 2 minutes or until crisp. Remove and drain on paper towel. Deep-fry the breast meat balls for 1½ minutes or until golden. Remove and drain on paper towel. Serve the leg meat and breast balls immediately.

SWEETCORN POLENTA

3 large cobs sweetcorn
100 g (3½ oz/⅔ cup) fine polenta
sea salt and freshly ground black pepper

Remove the husks from the corn and, using a large sharp knife, cut off the kernels as close as possible to the cobs. Place the cores in a large saucepan and reserve the kernels. Cover the cores with 1 litre (35 fl oz/4 cups) water and bring to the boil, then reduce the heat to low and simmer for 1 hour. Strain, discarding the solids. You will need 400 ml (14 fl oz) corn stock.

Meanwhile, juice the reserved kernels in a juicer. Pass through a fine sieve. Set aside.

Place the corn stock in a clean pan, bring to the boil over medium heat, then gradually whisk in the polenta until it is completely combined and thickened. Add the corn juice and continue to cook, stirring regularly, for 10 minutes. Pour into a deep 10 cm (4 inch) square tray and refrigerate until chilled and set. Using a 3 cm (1¼ inch) round cutter, cut 6 cylinders from the polenta.

PISTACHIO PURÉE

100 g (3½ oz/¾ cup) Iranian pistachio kernels
2 garlic cloves, finely chopped
finely grated zest of 1 orange
50 ml (1¾ fl oz) olive oil
20 ml (⅔ fl oz) vegetable oil

Blend all the ingredients in an upright blender with 40 ml (1¼ fl oz) water until smooth. Set aside.

ASPARAGUS AND CORN

1 cob sweetcorn
2 teaspoons olive oil
2 bunches thin asparagus, halved diagonally
sea salt and freshly ground black pepper

Remove the husk from the corn and, using a sharp knife, cut off the kernels as close as possible to the cob. Heat the oil in a saucepan over medium heat. Cook the kernels for 1 minute. Add the asparagus tips and cook for 1 minute. Season with salt and pepper. Set aside and keep warm.

CHICKEN JUS

150 ml (5 fl oz) chicken jus (see page 22)
2 teaspoons lemon juice

Heat the chicken jus and lemon juice in a small saucepan, stirring until warmed and combined. Set aside and keep warm.

PRESENTATION

30 g (1 oz/¼ cup) Iranian pistachio kernels, crushed

Spoon the pistachio purée onto 6 plates. Arrange a spatchcock ball and rectangle on top. Place the polenta alongside. Spoon over the asparagus and corn. Sauce with the chicken jus and scatter over the pistachios. Serves 6.

SEARED TUNA WITH TONKA BEAN MAYONNAISE, SMOKED POTATO AND JAMÓN CRUMBS

TONKA BEAN MAYONNAISE

1 egg yolk
10 g (⅓ oz) Dijon mustard
2 teaspoons lemon juice
2 teaspoons white wine vinegar
1 tonka bean, finely grated using a microplane grater
sea salt flakes
250 ml (9 fl oz/1 cup) olive oil
2 teaspoons Pernod Ricard or other pastis

Whisk together the egg yolk, mustard, lemon juice, vinegar, tonka bean and a pinch of salt in a bowl until thick and glossy. While whisking continuously, slowly drizzle in the oil and continue to whisk until thick and emulsified. Stir in the Pernod. Transfer to a 500 ml (17 fl oz/ 2 cup) cream canister and charge once. Set aside.

This can be made 1 day in advance and stored in the cream canister in the fridge. Bring to room temperature before serving.

SMOKED POTATO

5 large desiree potatoes, unpeeled
50 ml (1¾ fl oz) olive oil, plus extra for serving
sea salt flakes
30 g (1 oz) smoking chips

Preheat the oven to 160°C (315°F/Gas 2–3). Drizzle the potatoes with the oil and season with salt. Wrap each in foil and bake for 40 minutes or until cooked through. Remove from the oven and allow to cool.

Halve the potatoes lengthways. Using a tall 3 cm (1¼ inch) round cutter, cut 2 cylinders from each half. Choose the best 18 cylinders and discard the off-cuts.

Place the smoking chips in the bottom half of a steamer and the potato rounds in the top half. Place over high heat and once smoke appears, remove from the heat. Stand for 8 minutes or until the smoke has evaporated. Remove the potato and set aside.

When ready to serve, warm the potato in the oven, then drizzle with the oil.

JAMÓN CRUMBS

20 ml (⅔ fl oz) olive oil
2 eschalots (French shallots), finely diced
1 garlic clove, chopped
100 g (3½ oz) jamón Ibérico or other good-quality jamón, finely diced
200 g (7 oz/2½ cups) fresh breadcrumbs
½ bunch (70 g/2⅔ oz) flat-leaf (Italian) parsley, leaves picked and finely chopped
½ bunch (10 g/⅓ oz) chives, finely chopped

Heat the oil in a large frying pan over medium heat. Add the eschalot, garlic and jamón and cook for 10 minutes or until golden and crisp. Add the breadcrumbs and cook until crisp. Allow to cool, then stir through the herbs. Set aside.

TUNA

6 x 180 g (6½ oz) pieces of tuna fillet
sea salt and freshly ground black pepper

Remove any bloodline from the tuna and season with salt and pepper. Heat a frying pan over high heat. Once the pan is very hot, add the tuna and cook for 2 minutes. Turn the tuna, reduce the heat to medium and cook for another 2 minutes. Remove from the pan and rest in a warm place. Halve lengthways and serve immediately.

PRESENTATION

Place the tuna in the centre of 6 plates. Arrange 3 smoked potato rounds around the tuna. Place a generous spoonful of jamón crumbs beside the tuna and pipe the mayonnaise beside. Serves 6.

SLOW-COOKED PORK TENDERLOIN WITH QUINCE PURÉE, BROCCOLI AND PRUNE SAUCE

PORK TENDERLOIN

6 x 200 g (7 oz) pieces of pork tenderloin
sea salt flakes
60 ml (2 fl oz/¼ cup) extra virgin olive oil
20 ml (⅔ fl oz) olive oil

Heat a large saucepan of water to 63°C (145°F). Trim any excess sinew from the pork. Season with salt and place each in a small vacuum-seal or zip-lock bag with 2 teaspoons extra virgin olive oil. Follow the Masterclass on sous-vide cooking (see page 16) and cook for 1½ hours.

Preheat the oven to 180°C (350°F/Gas 4). Remove the pork from the bags. Heat the olive oil in an ovenproof frying pan over medium heat. Sear the pork all over, then roast for 4 minutes. Set aside and rest in a warm place. Thinly slice each piece widthways and serve immediately.

QUINCE PURÉE

2 large quinces
100 ml (3½ fl oz) olive oil
80 g (2¾ oz) caster (superfine) sugar
sea salt flakes

Peel the quinces and remove the cores. Coarsely chop the flesh and place in a saucepan with the oil. Cook over medium heat for 3 minutes, stirring occasionally. Add the sugar and enough water to just cover. Cook for 15 minutes or until the water is evaporated and the quince is tender, adding a little extra water, if necessary. Transfer to an upright blender and blend until smooth. Season with salt. Set aside and keep warm.

PRUNE SAUCE

100 g (3½ oz/½ cup) pitted prunes
40 ml (1¼ fl oz) sherry vinegar
1 fresh bay leaf
1 star anise
100 ml (3½ fl oz) veal jus (see page 24), warmed,
    approximately

Place the prunes, vinegar, bay leaf, star anise and 80 ml (2½ fl oz/⅓ cup) water in a saucepan and bring to the boil. Reduce the heat to low and simmer for 15 minutes. Remove the bay leaf and star anise and transfer to an upright blender. Add the warmed veal jus and blend until smooth. If needed, add more veal jus to thin the sauce. Pass through a fine sieve. Return to the pan and reheat ready to serve.

BROCCOLI

400 g (14 oz) broccoli
20 ml (⅔ fl oz) olive oil
sea salt and freshly ground black pepper

Remove the florets from the broccoli and discard. Trim one of the long sides of the stem so it is flat and, using a mandolin, slice lengthways into 1 mm (¹⁄₃₂ inch) thick slices. You will need 18 slices. Bring a small saucepan of water to the boil. Blanch the broccoli stem for 1 minute. Drain well and season with the oil, salt and pepper. Set aside and keep warm.

PRESENTATION

Spoon the quince purée onto 6 plates. Arrange the pork on the plate. Curl the broccoli stems and place around the plate. Spoon the prune sauce onto the plate. Serves 6.

BASS GROPER WITH SOUR ORANGE, MUSSELS, CLAMS AND MUSTARD PURÉE

DEHYDRATED BLACK OLIVE

200 g (7 oz/heaped 1½ cups) pitted black olives

Finely chop the olives and place on a baking tray lined with baking paper. Dry in a dehydrator at 60°C (140°F) for 3 hours. Alternatively, place in the oven on the lowest temperature and leave until completely dry.

This can be made 1 day in advance and stored in an airtight container in a dry place.

OLIVE, SESAME AND CHIVE CRUST

50 g (1¾ oz) dehydrated black olive
40 g (1½ oz/¼ cup) white sesame seeds
1 bunch (20 g/¾ oz) chives, finely chopped
finely grated zest of 1 lemon

Place all the ingredients in a bowl and combine. Set aside.

MUSTARD PURÉE

200 g (7 oz) dried chickpeas, soaked overnight, drained
50 g (1¾ oz) Dijon mustard
40 ml (1¼ fl oz) olive oil
sea salt and freshly ground black pepper

Place the chickpeas in a saucepan, cover with water and bring to a simmer. Cook for 1 hour or until completely tender. Strain, reserving a little of the cooking liquid.

Place the chickpeas in an upright blender, add the mustard and oil and blend until thick and smooth. Add a little reserved cooking liquid to thin down, if necessary. Season with salt and pepper. Set aside and keep warm.

DILL OIL

1 bunch (80 g/2¾ oz) dill, leaves picked
50 ml (1¾ fl oz) olive oil
sea salt flakes

Blend the dill and oil in an upright blender until smooth. Season with salt. Set aside.

MUSSELS AND CLAMS

300 ml (10½ fl oz) white wine
2 fresh bay leaves
4 sprigs thyme
10 g (⅓ oz) black peppercorns
500 g (1 lb 2 oz) black mussels, scrubbed
    and debearded
500 g (1 lb 2 oz) clams (vongole), purged and drained

Place half of each of the wine, bay leaves, thyme and peppercorns in a small saucepan and bring to the boil. Add the mussels, cover with a glass lid and cook until opened. As the mussels open, remove them from the pan and set aside. Discard the cooking liquid.

Repeat with the clams and remaining ingredients.

Remove the mussels and clams from their shells and set aside.

BORLOTTI BEANS

300 g (10½ oz) podded fresh borlotti beans
    (about 700 g/1 lb 9 oz unpodded)
½ brown onion
1 garlic clove
1 fresh bay leaf

Place all the ingredients in a saucepan, cover with water and bring to the boil. Reduce the heat to low and simmer until beans are tender. Remove from the heat and allow to cool in the liquid. Drain and set aside.

SOUR ORANGE SAUCE

1 litre (35 fl oz/4 cups) freshly squeezed orange juice
    (about 15 oranges)
2.5 g (1/12 oz) agar agar
2.5 g (1/12 oz) citric acid
2 g (1/16 oz) xanthan gum
150 ml (5 fl oz) extra virgin olive oil
1 quantity mussels and clams
1 quantity borlotti beans

Place the orange juice in a large saucepan over low heat and bring to a simmer. Cook for 20 minutes or until reduced to 250 ml (9 fl oz/1 cup). Increase the heat to high, add the agar agar and cook until the mixture reaches 90°C (194°F). Remove from the heat, transfer to a metal bowl and chill over ice until cool.

Transfer to an upright blender, add the citric acid, xanthan gum and oil and blend until smooth. Transfer to a clean pan and set aside.

When ready to serve, heat the sour orange sauce over medium heat, add the mussels, clams and borlotti beans and warm through.

BASS GROPER

1.2 kg (2 lb 10 oz) piece of bass groper fillet
sea salt and freshly ground black pepper
1 quantity olive, sesame and chive crust

Heat a large saucepan of water to 60°C (140°F).

Trim and cut the bass groper into 6 equal portions. Season with salt and pepper. Place each portion in a small vacuum-seal or zip-lock bag. Follow the Masterclass on sous vide (see page 16) and cook the fish for 12 minutes.

Remove the fish from the bags. Place the olive, sesame and chive crust on a plate and press one side of the bass groper into it. Serve immediately.

PRESENTATION

Spoon the sour orange sauce, mussels, clams and borlotti beans onto 6 plates. Place a piece of bass groper on top. Using 2 tablespoons, place a quenelle of purée next to the fish. Finish with a line of dill oil on the plate. Serves 6.

BABY SNAPPER WITH SWEETCORN, ZUCCHINI FLOWER, BLACK FUNGI AND SQUID INK

SQUID INK SAUCE

20 ml (⅔ fl oz) vegetable oil
1 carrot, coarsely chopped
1 onion, coarsely chopped
1 stalk celery, coarsely chopped
½ head garlic, cloves separated and chopped
1 sprig thyme
3 fresh bay leaves
250 ml (9 fl oz/1cup) fish stock (see page 23)
250 ml (9 fl oz/1cup) veal jus (see page 24)
40 ml (1¼ fl oz) squid ink

Heat the oil in a saucepan over medium–high heat. Cook the vegetables and garlic, stirring often, for 4 minutes or until golden. Add the thyme, bay leaves and stock. Simmer for 15 minutes or until reduced by half. Add the veal jus and simmer for 15 minutes or until reduced by half. Whisk in the squid ink and simmer for 5 minutes or until the sauce is thick enough to coat the back of a spoon. Pass through a fine sieve. Set aside and keep warm.

This can be made 1 day in advance and stored in an airtight container in the fridge. Reheat before serving.

SWEETCORN PURÉE

6 cobs sweetcorn
20 ml (⅔ fl oz) olive oil
40 g (1½ oz) unsalted butter
150 ml (5 fl oz) full-cream (whole) milk

Remove the husks from the corn and, using a large sharp knife, cut off the kernels as close as possible to the cobs. Set aside 100 g (3½ oz/½ cup) kernels for the vegetables.

Place the remaining kernels in a saucepan with the oil and butter. Cook over medium heat for 1 minute or until softened. Add the milk and simmer for 3 minutes. Transfer to an upright blender and blend until smooth. Pass through a fine sieve. Set aside and keep warm.

SWEETCORN, ZUCCHINI FLOWER AND BLACK FUNGI

12 zucchini (courgette) flowers (with baby
    zucchini attached)
200 g (7 oz) black fungi, woody core removed
100 g (3½ oz/½ cup) corn kernels (reserved from
    sweetcorn purée)
20 ml (⅔ fl oz) extra virgin olive oil
2 teaspoons lemon juice
sea salt and freshly ground black pepper

Remove the flowers from the baby zucchini and set aside for garnish. Halve the baby zucchini lengthways and place in a small saucepan with the black fungi, corn kernels and oil. Cook over medium heat for 1 minute. Season with the lemon juice, salt and pepper. Serve immediately.

SNAPPER

6 x 180 g (6½ oz) baby snapper fillets, skin on
sea salt and freshly ground white pepper
3 teaspoons olive oil

Season the snapper with salt and pepper. Heat a large non-stick frying pan over medium heat. Add the oil, then the snapper, skin-side down. Cook for 2 minutes or until the skin is crisp, then turn and cook for 10 seconds. Serve immediately.

PRESENTATION

zucchini flower petals, for garnish

Spoon the sweetcorn purée in a line onto 6 plates. Spoon the squid ink sauce in lines alongside. Scatter around some cooked vegetables and position a snapper fillet on top. Garnish with the zucchini flower petals. Serves 6.

ROASTED DUCK WITH MUSHROOM, CUTTLEFISH AND KOMBU GEL

MUSHROOMS

600 g (1 lb 5 oz) field mushrooms, trimmed
20 ml (⅔ fl oz) confit garlic oil (see page 25)
30 g (1 oz) confit garlic cloves, drained (see page 25)
30 g (1 oz) ground almonds (almond meal)
sea salt and freshly ground black pepper

Dice the mushrooms into 1 cm (½ inch) cubes. Place in a frying pan with the oil. Place over medium heat and cook until softened. Cool and spread over a baking tray lined with baking paper. Dry in a dehydrator at 60°C (140°F) for 3 hours. Alternatively, place in the oven on the lowest temperature and leave until completely dry.

Transfer to a food processor, add the confit garlic and ground almonds and process to form a crumb-like consistency. Season with salt and pepper. Set aside.

This can be made 1 day in advance and stored in an airtight container in the fridge. Bring to room temperature before serving.

KOMBU GEL

200 g (7 oz) dried kombu, rinsed and dried
20 ml (⅔ fl oz) rice vinegar
4 sheets gelatine, titanium strength

Place the kombu, vinegar and 500 ml (17 fl oz/2 cups) water in a small saucepan and bring to the boil. Set aside to infuse for 1 hour. Strain, then return the liquid to the pan.

Soak the gelatine in cold water for 5 minutes or until softened. Squeeze out the excess water, add the gelatine to the pan and place over medium heat, stirring until dissolved. Pour into a 15 x 10 cm (6 x 4 inch) container and refrigerate for 2 hours or until set.

This can be made 1 day in advance. When ready to serve, remove the gel from the container and, using a sharp knife, cut into 1 cm (½ inch) cubes.

ENDIVE

3 red endives
5 g (⅙ oz) ground nutmeg
10 g (⅓ oz) sea salt flakes

Heat a saucepan of water to 85°C (185°F). Halve the endives lengthways, sprinkle with the nutmeg and salt and place in a large vacuum-seal or zip-lock bag. Follow the Masterclass on sous vide (see page 16) and cook for 15 minutes. Remove from the water and bag and serve immediately.

144

VERJUICE SAUCE

200 ml (7 fl oz) verjuice
20 g (⅔ oz) ginger, sliced
10 g (⅓ oz) coriander seeds
0.3 g xanthan gum

Place the verjuice, ginger and coriander seeds in a small saucepan and bring to the boil. Remove from the heat and allow to infuse for 1 hour. Strain. Using a stick blender, blend in the xanthan gum until combined and the mixture has thickened. Set aside.

CUTTLEFISH

2 bunches enoki mushroom
100 g (3½ oz) cuttlefish, cleaned and wings removed
1 quantity verjuice sauce

Using kitchen scissors, trim the caps off the mushrooms and discard the stalks.

Using a sharp knife, finely score the cuttlefish, skin-side, in a criss-cross pattern. Slice into 5 mm (¼ inch) thick strips.

Place the mushroom caps, cuttlefish and verjuice sauce in a small saucepan over medium heat and cook until the cuttlefish is heated through and just beginning to curl. Set aside and keep warm.

DUCK BREAST

6 x 220 g (7¾ oz) duck breasts
sea salt and freshly ground black pepper

Preheat the oven to 170°C (325°F/Gas 3). Remove the excess sinew and fat from the duck breasts. Score the skin with a sharp knife and season with salt and pepper. Heat a large ovenproof frying pan over medium heat. Sear the duck, skin-side down, until golden, then place in the oven and roast for 6 minutes. Rest in a warm place for 5 minutes. Using a sharp knife, slice each breast lengthways into thin 2 mm (¹⁄₁₆ inch) thick strips. Arrange the slices, overlapping, then roll into a cylinder. Serve immediately.

PRESENTATION

Place a pile of mushrooms onto 6 plates. Place the duck cylinders on top and an endive half to one side. Scatter around the cuttlefish and enoki caps and 8–10 kombu gel cubes and finish with some of the verjuice sauce. Serves 6.

SLOW-COOKED BERKSHIRE PORK NECK WITH PINE MUSHROOMS AND PURPLE CONGO POTATO PURÉE

PORK NECK

1 x 1.2 kg (2 lb 10 oz) piece of Berkshire pork neck
90 ml (3 fl oz) olive oil
sea salt and freshly ground black pepper

Heat a saucepan of water to 59°C (138°C). Trim the excess fat from the pork and cut widthways into 6 equal portions. Season with salt and pepper. Place each in a small vacuum-seal or zip-lock bag with 3 teaspoons of oil. Follow the Masterclass on sous-vide cooking (see page 16) and cook the pork neck for 3½ hours. Remove the pork from the bags and thinly slice. Set aside and keep warm.

PINE MUSHROOMS AND BABY GLOBE ARTICHOKES

1 lemon
1 small brown onion, chopped
1 carrot, chopped
1 stalk celery, chopped
2 garlic cloves
3 fresh bay leaves
5 sprigs thyme
20 black peppercorns
300 ml (10½ fl oz) white wine
50 ml (1¾ fl oz) white wine vinegar
12 baby globe artichokes
sea salt and freshly ground black pepper
30 ml (1 fl oz) extra virgin olive oil
400 g (14 oz) pine mushrooms, trimmed and sliced

Using a small sharp knife, remove the peel of the lemon, then remove the white pith from the peel. Juice the remaining lemon and place the juice and squeezed halves in a large bowl of water. Set aside.

Place the vegetables, garlic, herbs, peppercorns, wine, vinegar, lemon zest and 1.5 litres (52 fl oz) water in a large saucepan and bring to the boil.

Meanwhile, working with one artichoke at a time, remove the outer leaves, trim the top and peel the stem, then place in the acidulated water — this will keep it from discolouring. Once all the artichokes are prepared, drain

and add to the pan. Allow the pan to return to the boil, then reduce the heat to low and simmer for 6 minutes. Remove from the heat and allow the artichokes to cool in the liquid. Remove the artichokes and halve.

Heat the oil in a saucepan over medium heat. Cook the mushrooms for 3 minutes or until softened. Season with salt and pepper and toss through the artichokes. Set aside and keep warm.

PURPLE CONGO POTATO PURÉE

500 g (1 lb 2 oz) purple congo potato
3 garlic cloves, finely grated
finely grated zest of 1 orange
80 ml (2½ fl oz/⅓ cup) extra virgin olive oil
40 ml (1¼ fl oz) Forum chardonnay vinegar

Peel, then chop the potato into equal pieces, place in a saucepan of cold water and bring to the boil. Reduce the heat to low and simmer until cooked through. Drain and transfer to a food processor with the remaining ingredients and process until smooth. Pass through a fine sieve. Set aside and keep warm.

WALNUT JUS

150 ml (5 fl oz) veal jus (see page 24)
20 ml (⅔ fl oz) walnut oil
18 walnuts halves, roasted

Heat the veal jus in a small saucepan. Add the walnut oil and walnuts. Set aside and keep warm.

PRESENTATION

fennel pollen, for garnish

Arrange the pork neck onto plates. Using 2 tablespoons, place a quenelle of purée alongside. Spoon over the mushrooms and artichokes and drizzle over the walnut jus. Garnish with the fennel pollen. Serves 6

CELERIAC, MUSHROOM AND ALMOND 'CANNELLONI' WITH SAFFRON ESCHALOTS

ALMOND SAUCE

200 g (7 oz/1⅓ cups) blanched almonds
100 ml (3½ fl oz) almond oil
200 ml (7 fl oz) full-cream (whole) milk
6 g (⅕ oz) xanthan gum
sea salt and freshly ground white pepper

Place the almonds and oil in an upright blender and blend until smooth. Pass through a fine sieve, discarding the solids. Transfer to a saucepan over low heat and gradually whisk in the milk. Add the xanthan gum and stir for about 1 minute or until thickened and emulsified. Season with salt and pepper. Set aside and keep warm.

This can be made 1 day in advance and stored in an airtight container in the fridge. Reheat before serving.

MUSHROOM FILLING

100 ml (3½ fl oz) olive oil
2 brown onions, thinly sliced
2 garlic cloves, thinly sliced
20 saffron threads
500 g (1 lb 2 oz) field mushrooms, trimmed
200 g (7 oz/2½ cups) fresh breadcrumbs

Heat half the oil in a saucepan over medium heat. Add the onion and garlic and cook for 10 minutes or until the onion is translucent. Add the saffron and cook for 10 minutes or until the onion is softened. Keep warm.

Meanwhile, dice the mushrooms into 1 cm (½ inch) cubes. Heat the remaining oil in a frying pan over medium heat. Cook the mushrooms for 5 minutes or until softened. Drain, then add to the onion mixture. Stir in the breadcrumbs and cool to room temperature.

DUTCH CARROTS

20 ml (⅔ fl oz) extra virgin olive oil
6 dutch carrots, trimmed and halved widthways

Heat the oil in a small frying pan over medium heat. Cook the carrots for 4 minutes or until just cooked through. Set aside and keep warm.

CELERIAC 'CANNELLONI'

1 large celeriac (about 700 g/1 lb 9 oz)

Bring a saucepan of salted water to the boil. Using a knife, trim the top and base of the celeriac and peel the sides. Using a mandolin, slice the celeriac lengthways into 1 mm (1/32 inch) thick slices. Blanch the slices for 30 seconds, drain, then refresh in iced water and drain again.

Arrange 3–4 celeriac slices overlapping each other on a sheet of plastic wrap to form a 15 cm (6 inch) square. Repeat to make 6 squares. Discard any remaining celeriac. Place the mushroom filling in the centre of each square and roll up to form cylinders. Roll the plastic wrap up tightly and tie the ends to secure.

These can be made 1 day in advance and stored in an airtight container in the fridge. When ready to serve, heat a large saucepan of water to 90°C (194°F) and poach the cylinders for 10 minutes. Scoop out, remove the plastic wrap and serve immediately.

SAFFRON ESCHALOTS

20 ml (2/3 fl oz) extra virgin olive oil
6 small eschalots (French shallots)
1 cinnamon stick
10 g (1/3 oz) coriander seeds
4 cardamom pods, bruised
20 saffron threads
200 ml (7 fl oz) freshly squeezed orange juice (about 3 oranges)

Place the oil and eschalots in a small saucepan over medium heat. Cook for 3 minutes or until golden. Add the spices and juice, reduce the heat to low–medium and cook for 20 minutes or until reduced to a thickened glaze which coats the eschalots. Set aside and keep warm.

PRESENTATION

40 g (1½ oz/¼ cup) blanched almonds, toasted

Pound the almonds using a mortar and pestle until finely crushed. Coat the 'cannelloni' in the almond sauce, place onto 6 plates and sprinkle over the crushed almond. Arrange the carrot and eschalots alternately around the plate. Serves 6.

BLACK OLIVE PURÉE

200 g (7 oz) Kalamata olives, pitted
50 ml (1½ fl oz) extra virgin olive oil

Place olives in a small saucepan, cover with water and bring to the boil, then drain. Transfer to an upright blender, add the oil and blend until smooth. Pass through a fine sieve.
This can be made 2 days in advance and stored in an airtight container in the fridge.

SQUID INK CRUMBS

50 g (1¾ oz) unsalted butter
50 g (1¾ oz) plain (all-purpose) flour
20 ml (⅔ fl oz) squid ink
1 teaspoon harissa spice mix (see page 75)
20 g (¾ oz) black olive purée

Preheat the oven to 160°C (315°F/Gas 2–3). Using your hands, rub the butter and flour together to form coarse crumbs. Add the squid ink and spice mix and mix until a dough forms. Place between baking paper and roll out to 5 mm (¼ inch) thick. Place on a baking tray, remove the top sheet of paper and bake for 15 minutes or until crisp. Cool on the tray. Crush into small pieces using a mortar and pestle and fold through the purée. Set aside.
These can be made 1 day in advance and stored in an airtight container.

POTATO-YOGHURT PURÉE

200 g (7 oz) desiree potato, unpeeled
75 g (2¾ oz) unsalted butter, softened
50 g (1¾ oz) arrowroot
100 g (3½ oz) Greek yoghurt

Place the potato in a saucepan of cold water, bring to the boil and cook until tender. Drain and remove the skin. Pass through a food mill (mouli or ricer) or drum sieve (tamis). Fold in the butter and arrowroot, then whisk in the yoghurt until smooth. Set aside and keep warm.

HAPUKA

6 x 180 g (6½ oz) hapuka fillets
sea salt flakes
60 ml (2 fl oz/¼ cup) extra virgin olive oil

Heat a large saucepan of water to 61°C (142°F). Sprinkle the fish with salt and place each in a small vacuum-seal or zip-lock bag with 2 teaspoons oil. Follow the Masterclass on sous-vide cooking (see page 16) and cook the fish for 14 minutes. Remove from the water and rest in the bags for 2 minutes. Remove from the bags, reserving the juices. Serve immediately.

HERB EMULSION

140 g (5 oz/2 bunches) coriander (cilantro),
    leaves picked
20 g (⅔ oz) flat-leaf (Italian) parsley, leaves picked
50 ml (1¾ fl oz) extra virgin olive oil
hapuka cooking juices
2 teaspoons lemon juice
sea salt and freshly ground black pepper

Bring a saucepan of water to the boil. Blanch the herbs for 1 minute. Drain, then refresh in iced water. Drain again. Transfer to an upright blender, add the oil and blend until smooth. Pass through a fine sieve. Gradually whisk in the hapuka cooking juices until combined. Season with lemon juice, salt and pepper. Gently reheat to serve.

BABY GLOBE ARTICHOKE AND SAMPHIRE

1 lemon
½ brown onion, chopped
1 carrot, chopped
1 stalk celery, chopped
2 garlic cloves
3 fresh bay leaves
5 sprigs thyme
20 black peppercorns
300 ml (10½ fl oz) white wine
50 ml (1¾ fl oz) white wine vinegar
12 baby globe artichokes
100 g (3½ oz) samphire
30 ml (1 fl oz) herb emulsion
sea salt flakes

Using a small sharp knife, remove the peel of the lemon, then remove the white pith from the peel. Juice the lemon and place the juice and squeezed halves in a large bowl of water. Set aside.

Place the vegetables, garlic, herbs, peppercorns, wine, vinegar and lemon peel in a large saucepan, add 1.5 litres (52 fl oz) water and bring to the boil.

Meanwhile, working with one artichoke at a time, remove the outer leaves, trim the top and peel the stem, then place in the acidulated water — this will keep it from discolouring. Drain, add to the pan and allow the pan to return to the boil, then reduce the heat and simmer for 6 minutes. Remove from the heat and allow the artichokes to cool in the liquid. Halve the artichokes and combine with the samphire and herb emulsion and season with salt. Set aside and keep warm.

PRESENTATION

2 sprigs dill, leaves picked and finely chopped

Place the potato-yoghurt purée in the centre of 6 plates and top with the hapuka. Toss the artichokes and samphire in the dill and distribute between the plates. Scatter over the crumbs. Serves 6.

This isn't a mayonnaise in the traditional sense as it doesn't contain egg yolks. The
texture, however, always reminds me of mayonnaise. Most people would associate 'burnt'
with 'bitter', but burnt onions have a balanced sweetness that adds a depth of flavour

BRAISED WAGYU BEEF CHEEK WITH
BURNT ONION 'MAYONNAISE' AND KALE

WAGYU BEEF CHEEKS

30 ml (1 fl oz) vegetable oil
1 onion, roughly chopped
1 stalk celery, roughly chopped
1 carrot, roughly chopped
½ capsicum (pepper), roughly chopped
½ head garlic
3 star anise
1 cinnamon stick
12 g (⅖ oz) coriander seeds
200 ml (7 fl oz) soy sauce
1.2 litres (42 fl oz) veal jus (see page 24)
400 ml (14 fl oz) white chicken stock (see page 22)
finely grated zest of 1 orange
1 long red chilli, halved
50 g (1¾ oz) honey
100 ml (3½ fl oz) olive oil
6 x 300 g (10½ oz) wagyu beef cheeks, trimmed

Preheat the oven to 160°C (315°F/Gas 2–3). Heat the vegetable oil in a large saucepan over medium heat. Add the vegetables and garlic and cook for 3–4 minutes or until golden. Add the spices and cook for 1–2 minutes. Add the soy sauce, jus, stock, orange zest, chilli and honey and bring to the boil. Set aside. Heat the olive oil in a large frying pan over high heat. Sear the cheeks until browned all over. Place in the braising liquid, cover with a cartouche, then a lid and bake for 3 hours or until a skewer inserted into the meat meets no resistance.

Take 400 ml (14 fl oz) liquid from the pan and strain. Place in a clean pan and simmer for 10 minutes or until reduced by half. Set aside and keep warm. When ready to serve, remove the cheeks from the liquid and serve hot.

BURNT ONION 'MAYONNAISE'

3 brown onions, unpeeled
110 ml (3⅔ fl oz) vegetable oil
1 head garlic, halved widthways

2 fresh bay leaves
10 g (⅓ oz/½ bunch) thyme
350 ml (12 fl oz) white chicken stock (see page 22)
1 g (1/32 oz) xanthan gum

Halve 2 onions and place, cut-side down, in a frying pan with 2 teaspoons oil. Cook over high heat, without turning, for 3 minutes or until blackened. Remove from the pan and set aside. Repeat with the garlic using the same pan.

Peel the remaining onion and thinly slice. Heat 2 teaspoons oil in a large frying pan over high heat. Cook the sliced onion for 3 minutes, allowing it to scorch and 'catch' on the base of the pan. Add the burnt onion halves and garlic, herbs, stock and 350 ml (12 fl oz) water to the pan, reduce the heat to low and simmer for 3 hours.

Strain and return the liquid to a clean pan over medium heat. Simmer for 15 minutes or until reduced to 100 ml (3½ fl oz), skimming the scum from the surface regularly. Remove from the heat. Add the xanthan gum and the remaining oil and process using a stick blender until emulsified. Set aside and keep warm.

KALE

200 g (7 oz) purple kale
20 ml (⅔ fl oz) extra virgin olive oil

Pick the kale leaves, discarding the stems. Heat a frying pan over medium heat. Add the oil, then the kale and cook for 2 minutes or until just wilted. Serve immediately.

PRESENTATION

Spoon the mayonnaise onto 6 plates and place a cheek to one side of it. Arrange some of the cooked kale around the cheek. Sauce the cheek with the reduced braising liquid. Serves 6.

POACHED CHICKEN
WITH SAFFRON ESCHALOTS,
HERB EMULSION
AND JAMÓN CRUMBS

POACHED CHICKEN

3 x 1 kg (2 lb 4 oz) whole free-range chickens
sea salt and freshly ground black pepper
1 sprig thyme, leaves picked
60 ml (2 fl oz/¼ cup) olive oil
15 g (½ oz) coriander seeds, toasted and ground
7 g (¼ oz) cumin seeds, toasted and ground

Remove the legs from the chickens and set aside.

Remove the breast fillets, then remove the skin and discard. Season with salt, pepper, thyme and oil. Place each breast in a small vacuum-seal or zip-lock bag and set aside.

Remove the bones from the legs. Using a boning knife, make an incision on the inside of each leg, folding the thigh and leg bone in an L shape and cutting right down to the bone. Carefully cut the flesh away from the bone, then remove the bone, making sure to keep the skin intact. Lay the leg meat, skin-side down, flat on a board. Combine the ground coriander and cumin and sprinkle over the legs. Season with salt and pepper. Working with one leg at a time, push the meat together to form a rough square, then roll widthways to form a cylinder. Roll tightly in plastic wrap and tie the ends to secure.

Heat a large saucepan of water to 68°C (154°F), then add the leg meat cylinders. Meanwhile, follow the Masterclass on sous-vide cooking (see page 16) to seal the bags with the breasts in them. Once the leg meat has been cooking for 35 minutes, add the breasts to the water and continue cooking for 8 minutes. Remove all the chicken and rest for 5 minutes.

Remove the breasts from the bags, place on a board and trim to form a rectangular shape, then halve each lengthways.

Remove the plastic wrap from the leg meat, then cut each into 2 equal pieces. Set aside and keep warm.

JAMÓN CRUMBS

20 ml (⅔ fl oz) olive oil
2 eschalots (French shallots), finely diced
1 garlic clove, chopped
100 g (3½ oz) jamón Ibérico or other good-quality jamón, finely diced
200 g (7 oz/2½ cups) fresh breadcrumbs

Heat the oil in a large frying pan over medium heat. Add the eschalot, garlic and jamón and cook for 10 minutes or until golden and crisp. Add the breadcrumbs and cook until crisp. Allow to cool and set aside.

SAFFRON ESCHALOTS

20 ml (⅔ fl oz) extra virgin olive oil
12 small eschalots (French shallots), halved if large
1 cinnamon stick
10 g (⅓ oz) coriander seeds
4 cardamom pods, bruised
20 saffron threads
200 ml (7 fl oz) freshly squeezed orange juice (about 3 oranges)

Place the oil and eschalots in a small saucepan over medium heat. Cook for 3 minutes or until golden. Add the spices and juice, reduce the heat to medium–low and cook for 20 minutes or until reduced to a thickened glaze which coats the eschalots. Set aside and keep warm.

HERB EMULSION

2 bunches (160 g/5¾ oz) coriander (cilantro), leaves picked
1 bunch (150 g/5½ oz) flat-leaf (Italian) parsley, leaves picked
50 ml (1¾ fl oz) extra virgin olive oil
sea salt and freshly ground black pepper

Bring a saucepan of water to the boil. Blanch the herbs for 1 minute. Drain, then refresh in iced water. Drain again. Transfer to an upright blender, add the oil and blend until smooth. Pass through a fine sieve. Season with salt and pepper. Set aside.

PRESENTATION

Spoon the herb emulsion in lines onto 6 plates. Arrange the poached chicken breast and leg meat on top. Place eschalots alongside and place a pile of jamón crumbs on the plate. Serves 6.

ROASTED BLACK ANGUS SIRLOIN WITH SMOKED LEEK, BLACK FUNGI AND KOHLRABI PURÉE

LEEKS

4 leeks

Remove the green tops and roots of the leeks. Rinse the white stalk, then wrap 2 leeks each in foil and place on a gas flame or electric element over medium–high heat. Cook for about 6 minutes, using tongs to carefully turn the leeks every 2 minutes. Unwrap the leeks — the outer layers should be blackened and the inside tender. Set aside to cool. Peel off the blackened layers and discard. Cut each leek widthways into 3 pieces.

These can be prepared up to 1 day in advance and stored in an airtight container in the fridge. Reheat the leeks in a steamer before serving.

RED WINE SAUCE

1 small onion
1 small carrot
1 stalk celery
20 ml (⅔ fl oz) olive oil
½ head garlic, halved widthways
5 whole allspice
2 star anise
5 g (⅛ oz) black peppercorns
2 fresh bay leaves
10 g (⅓ oz/½ bunch) thyme
250 ml (9 fl oz/1 cup) red wine
200 ml (7 fl oz) veal jus (see page 24)

Roughly dice the onion, carrot and celery. Heat the oil in a saucepan over medium heat. Add the vegetables and garlic and cook for 4 minutes or until caramelised. Add the spices and herbs and cook for 1 minute. Deglaze the pan with the wine and cook for 12 minutes or until the sauce is reduced by three-quarters and is a thick glaze. Add the veal jus and cook for 15 minutes or until the sauce is reduced by one-third, skimming the scum from the surface regularly. Strain, discarding the solids. Set aside and keep warm.

This can be made 1 day in advance and stored in an airtight container in the fridge.

BLACK FUNGI

20 ml (⅔ fl oz) olive oil
100 g (3½ oz) black fungi, woody core removed
sea salt and freshly ground black pepper

Heat a frying pan over high heat. Add the oil, then the fungi and cook for 1 minute. Season with salt and pepper.

KOHLRABI PURÉE

2 heads kohlrabi (about 400 g/14 oz in total)
450 ml (16 fl oz) full-cream (whole) milk, or to cover
sea salt and freshly ground white pepper

Peel the kohlrabi and cut into 2 cm (¾ inch) dice. Place in a saucepan and add enough milk to cover. Bring to the boil, then reduce the heat to low and simmer until cooked through. Strain, reserving both the solids and milk. Transfer the kohlrabi to an upright blender and blend, adding just enough reserved milk to form a thick, smooth purée. Season with salt and pepper. Set aside and keep warm.

BLACK ANGUS SIRLOIN

1.2 kg (2 lb 10 oz) piece of black angus sirloin
30 ml (1 fl oz) vegetable oil

Preheat the oven to 180°C (350°F/Gas 4). Trim the excess fat from the beef. Halve the sirloin lengthways, then cut each piece widthways into 3 equal pieces so you have 6 x 200 g (7 oz) portions. Heat the oil in a large ovenproof frying pan. Sear the beef until browned all over. Place the pan in the oven and roast for 3 minutes, then turn the beef over and roast for another 3 minutes for medium-rare. Rest in a warm place until required. When ready to serve, carve each piece in half diagonally.

PRESENTATION

Place 2 pieces of sirloin at opposite ends of 6 plates. Spoon the kohlrabi purée between the pieces of sirloin. Place a piece of leek beside each sirloin. Scatter the fungi next to the sirloin and finish with the red wine sauce. Serves 6.

ROASTED MANDAGERY CREEK VENISON WITH SPICED BEETROOT PURÉE AND MUSHROOMS

SPICE MIX

20 g (⅔ oz) coriander seeds
20 g (⅔ oz) cumin seeds
5 g (⅙ oz) whole allspice

Preheat the oven to 170°C (325°F/Gas 3). Roast the spices for 8 minutes. Grind using a spice grinder, then pass through a fine sieve.

SMOKED BEETROOT

6 beetroot (about 900 g/2 lb in total), scrubbed and trimmed
30 g (1 oz) smoking chips
olive oil, for drizzling

Preheat the oven to 170°C (325°F/Gas 3). Wrap each beetroot in foil and bake for 1½ hours or until tender. When cool enough to handle, peel and cut twelve 2 cm (¾ inch) cubes from each beetroot, reserving the off-cuts for the beetroot purée.

Place the smoking chips in the bottom half of a steamer and the beetroot cubes in the top half. Place over high heat and once smoke appears, remove from the heat. Stand for 8 minutes or until the smoke has evaporated. Remove the beetroot and set aside.

When ready to serve, warm in the oven and drizzle with olive oil.

BEETROOT PURÉE

roasted beetroot off-cuts (reserved from smoked beetroot)
60 g (2 oz/¼ cup) Greek yoghurt
30 ml (1 fl oz) olive oil
2 teaspoons balsamic vinegar
1 quantity spice mix
sea salt and freshly ground black pepper

Place the beetroot, yoghurt, oil, vinegar and spice mix in an upright blender and blend until smooth. Season with salt and pepper. Pass through a fine sieve. Set aside and keep warm.

DEHYDRATED MUSHROOMS

300 g (10½ oz) field mushrooms, trimmed
40 ml (1¼ fl oz) confit garlic oil (see page 25)
sea salt and freshly ground black pepper

Dice the mushrooms into 1 cm (½ inch) cubes. Heat 30 ml (1 fl oz) garlic oil in a frying pan over medium heat. Add the mushrooms, season with salt and pepper and cook until softened. Drain and place on a baking tray lined with baking paper. Dry in a dehydrator at 60°C (140°F) for 1 hour. Alternatively, place in the oven on the lowest temperature and leave until completely dry. When ready to serve, heat the remaining garlic oil in a small frying pan over low heat and warm the dehydrated mushrooms.

HORSERADISH PURÉE

30 ml (1 fl oz) olive oil
100 g (3½ oz) fresh horseradish, peeled and finely grated
1 garlic clove, chopped
200 ml (7 fl oz) full-cream (whole) milk
20 ml (⅔ fl oz) Forum chardonnay vinegar
sea salt and freshly ground black pepper

Heat the oil in a saucepan over medium heat. Add the horseradish and garlic and cook for 2 minutes. Add the milk and cook for 15 minutes or until the horseradish is softened. Transfer to an upright blender and blend until smooth. Add the vinegar, season with salt and pepper and blend until combined. Pass through a fine sieve. Set aside and keep warm.

VENISON

6 x 200 g (7 oz) pieces of Mandagery Creek venison loin
sea salt and freshly ground black pepper
20 ml (⅔ fl oz) olive oil

Preheat the oven to 180°C (350°F/Gas 4). Heat an ovenproof frying pan over high heat. Season the venison with salt and pepper. Add the oil to the pan, then the venison and sear on all sides. Place in the oven and roast for 2 minutes, then turn over, season again, and roast for another 2 minutes. Rest in a warm place for 6–10 minutes.

When ready to serve, return the venison to the oven for 1 minute. Remove from the oven and halve each piece widthways. Serve immediately.

PRESENTATION

15 g (½ oz) freeze-dried beetroot powder (see Note)

Spoon the beetroot purée onto 6 plates and place the venison pieces on top. Scatter the dehydrated mushrooms around and place 2 beetroot cubes alongside. Dot the horseradish purée around the plate and sprinkle with the beetroot powder. Serves 6.

NOTE This is available from health food stores and gourmet food stores.

WARM POTATO AND ALMOND NOUGAT WITH BLACK TRUFFLE SAUCE AND PINE MUSHROOM

DEHYDRATED BLACK OLIVE

200 g (7 fl oz/heaped 1½ cups) pitted black olives

Finely chop the olives and place on a baking tray lined with baking paper. Dry in a dehydrator at 60°C (140°F) for 3 hours. Alternatively, place in the oven on the lowest temperature and leave until completely dry.

This can be made 1 day in advance and stored in an airtight container in a dry place.

POTATO AND ALMOND NOUGAT

140 g (5 oz) desiree potatoes
120 ml (4 fl oz) olive oil
750 ml (26 fl oz/3 cups) full-cream (whole) milk
150 g (5½ oz/1½ cups) ground almonds (almond meal)
10 g (⅓ oz) agar agar
10 g (⅓ oz) methylcelullose
2 g (¹⁄₁₆ oz) xanthan gum
50 g (1¾ oz) deyhydrated black olive

Peel the potatoes and dice into 5 mm (¼ inch) cubes. Place in a small saucepan, cover with the oil and place over low heat. Cook for 10 minutes or until tender. Drain and set aside.

Place the milk and ground almonds in a saucepan and bring to the boil. Remove from the heat and set aside for 10 minutes to infuse. Transfer to a food processor and process until smooth. Pass through a fine sieve into a clean pan and place over medium heat. Add the agar agar and heat to 90°C (194°F) for 1 minute, then remove from the heat.

Use a stick blender to blend the mixture and while blending, gradually add the methylcellulose and xanthan gum and blend until combined. Stir through the potato and dehydrated black olive, then place in the freezer and cool to 1–4°C (34–39°F).

Lay a sheet of plastic wrap on a work surface. Divide the chilled nougat into 6 equal portions. Take the first portion and form into a 4 cm (1½ inch) wide log in the centre of the plastic wrap. Using the plastic wrap as a guide, roll the nougat into a cylinder and tie off the ends tightly to secure. Repeat with the remaining nougat. Refrigerate until ready to serve.

This can be made 1 day in advance. When ready to serve, heat a saucepan of water to 90°C (194°F). Poach the nougat cylinders for 10 minutes or until warmed through. Scoop out and remove the plastic wrap. Using a sharp knife, trim the ends, then cut each widthways into 3 pieces.

BLACK TRUFFLE SAUCE

1 brown onion, chopped
2 garlic cloves, chopped
2 teaspoons olive oil
200 g (7 oz) fresh black truffle, finely chopped (see Note)
30 ml (1 fl oz) good-quality truffle oil (see Note)
3 g (1/10 oz) xanthan gum

Place the onion, garlic and oil in a saucepan over medium heat and cook until softened. Add 200 ml (7 fl oz) water, and continue to cook for 15 minutes. Add the truffle and truffle oil, reduce the heat to low and simmer for 10 minutes to infuse. Remove from the heat. Using a stick blender, blend until combined and smooth. While blending, gradually add the xanthan gum and blend until combined. Set aside in a warm place.

NOTE Fresh black truffle and truffle oil are available from gourmet food stores.

PINE MUSHROOM, SALSIFY AND BABY LEEK

0.5 g citric acid
500 g (1 lb 2 oz) salsify (oyster plant)
½ brown onion, chopped
1 carrot, chopped
1 stalk celery, chopped
1 garlic clove
1 fresh bay leaf
1 sprig thyme
5 black peppercorns
75 ml (2⅔ fl oz) white wine
3 teaspoons white wine vinegar
peel of ½ lemon, white pith removed
6 pine mushrooms
30 ml (1 fl oz) olive oil
18 baby leeks, trimmed
sea salt flakes

Fill a large plastic container with 1 litre (35 fl oz/4 cups) water and add the citric acid. Peel the salsify and place in the acidulated water — this will keep them from discolouring. Place the onion, carrot, celery, garlic, bay leaf, thyme, peppercorns, wine, vinegar and lemon peel with 325 ml (11 fl oz) water in a large saucepan and bring to the boil. Drain the salsify, add to the pan, return to the boil, then reduce the heat to low and simmer for 10 minutes. Remove from the heat and allow the salsify to cool in the stock. Cut the salsify into small pieces and set aside.

Quarter the pine mushrooms, place in a saucepan over medium heat with the oil and cook for 2–3 minutes. Add the leeks and cook for 1 minute. Set aside and keep warm.

PRESENTATION

Place 2 pieces of nougat on a tray and spoon over the truffle sauce to coat, then place on plates. Spoon some truffle sauce on the plate and stand a piece of uncoated nougat on top. Arrange the salsify, mushrooms and baby leek around the plate. Serves 6.

ROASTED KING SALMON WITH WHITE ASPARAGUS, ROASTED BEETROOT AND TURNIP

BEETROOT GEL

2 large beetroot (about 500 g/1 lb 2 oz in total)
500 ml (17 fl oz/2 cups) white chicken stock (see page 22)
2 teaspoons balsamic vinegar
3 garlic cloves
6 g (⅕ oz) coriander seed
2 g (1/16 oz) cumin seeds
0.5 g whole allspice
15 black peppercorns
1 cinnamon stick
1 star anise
1 fresh bay leaf
10 g (⅓ oz/½ bunch) thyme
sea salt flakes
5 g (⅙ oz) agar agar

Peel and thinly slice the beetroot. Place in a large saucepan, add the stock, vinegar, garlic, spices, herbs and 500 ml (17 fl oz/2 cups) water and bring to the boil. Reduce the heat to low and simmer for 2 hours. Strain, discarding the solids. Return the liquid to the pan and simmer until reduced to 500 ml (17 fl oz/2 cups). Season with salt. Add the agar agar and cook, stirring continuously until dissolved. Transfer to a metal bowl and place over ice until set. Transfer the gel to an upright blender and blend until smooth. Pass through a fine sieve and set aside.

This can be made 1 day in advance and stored in an airtight container in the fridge.

ROASTED BEETROOT AND TURNIP

6 baby red beetroot
6 baby golden beetroot
6 baby turnips
juice of 1 lemon
60 ml (2 fl oz/¼ cup) olive oil

Preheat the oven to 170°C (325°F/Gas 3). Wrap the red beetroot together in foil and repeat with the golden beetroot. Roast both for 30 minutes.

Meanwhile, peel the turnips, place in the top half of a steamer placed over simmering water and cook for 10–12 minutes. Quarter and dress with a little lemon juice and oil.

Peel the red roasted beetroot. Quarter and dress with a little lemon juice and oil. Repeat

WHITE ASPARAGUS

18 spears white asparagus
20 ml (⅔ fl oz) olive oil

Trim the ends of the asparagus and halve widthways. Place in a frying pan with the oil over low heat and cook until tender. Set aside and keep warm.

ROASTED KING SALMON

1.2 kg (2 lb 10 oz) piece of king salmon fillet, skin on and pin-boned
90 ml (3 fl oz) olive oil
200 ml (7 fl oz) vegetable oil
sea salt and freshly ground black pepper

Remove the skin from the salmon and refrigerate the fillet until required. Rinse and remove any scales from the skin. Place on a baking tray lined with baking paper and dry in a dehydrator at 60°C (140°F) for 5 hours. Alternatively, place in the oven on the lowest temperature and leave until completely dry.

Meanwhile, heat a saucepan of water to 68°C (154°F). Cut the fillet into 6 equal portions. Place each in a small vacuum-seal or zip-lock bag with 3 teaspoons olive oil. Follow the Masterclass on sous-vide cooking (see page 16) and cook the fish for 4 minutes, then remove from the bags and keep warm.

When ready to serve, heat the vegetable oil to 180°C (350°F). Cut the dehydrated skin into 3 cm (1¼ inch) squares and deep-fry for 1 minute or until bubbled and crisp. Remove and drain on paper towel. Using a sharp knife, slice into 3 mm (⅛ inch) thick strips. Season with salt and pepper and serve immediately.

PRESENTATION

½ bunch (10 g/⅓ oz) chives, finely chopped

Place the salmon on 6 plates. Arrange the beetroot and turnip around the salmon and place some asparagus tips in between. Dip one end of the asparagus stalks in the chives and place on the plates. Dot the plate with the beetroot gel and garnish with pieces of crisp salmon skin. Serves 6.

SLOW-COOKED LAMB RUMP WITH KIPFLER POTATO AND HAZELNUT

SLOW-COOKED LAMB

6 x 220 g (7¾ oz) lamb rumps
sea salt flakes
60 ml (2 fl oz/¼ cup) extra virgin olive oil

Heat a large saucepan of water to 63°C (145°F). Trim any excess sinew from the lamb. Sprinkle with salt and place each piece in a small vacuum-seal or zip-lock bag with 2 teaspoons oil. Follow the Masterclass on sous vide (see page 16) and cook the lamb for 3 hours.

When ready to serve, preheat the oven to 180°C (350°F/Gas 4). Remove the lamb from the bags and place, fat-side down, in a large ovenproof frying pan over high heat and sear all over. Place in the oven and roast for 4 minutes. Rest in a warm place.

PARMESAN CRUMBS

40 g (1½ oz) unsalted butter
40 g (1½ oz) plain (all-purpose) flour
40 g (1½ oz) finely grated parmesan
10 g (⅓ oz) hazelnuts, roasted and roughly chopped
sea salt flakes

Preheat the oven to 160°C (315°F/Gas 2–3). Rub the butter and flour together to form crumbs. Add the parmesan and hazelnuts and knead together to form a dough. Roll out between baking paper to 5 mm (¼ inch) thick. Place on a baking tray, remove the top sheet of paper and bake for 16 minutes or until crisp. Allow to cool. Break to form large crumbs.

These can be made 1 day in advance and stored in an airtight container.

HAZELNUT PURÉE

200 g (7 oz) hazelnuts, roasted and skins removed
150 ml (5 fl oz) full-cream (whole) milk
20 ml (⅔ fl oz) sherry vinegar
3 confit garlic cloves (see page 25)
juice of ½ lemon
30 ml (1 fl oz) vegetable oil
sea salt flakes

Place the hazelnuts and milk in a saucepan over low heat and cook for 20 minutes. Transfer to an upright blender, add the remaining ingredients and blend until smooth. Pass through a fine sieve. Season with salt and keep warm.

This can be made 1 day in advance and stored in an airtight container in the fridge. Reheat before serving.

KIPFLER POTATO AND ZUCCHINI

300 g (10½ oz) kipfler potato
20 g (⅔ oz) unsalted butter
30 ml (1 fl oz) olive oil
sea salt and freshly ground black pepper
6 zucchini (courgette) flowers (with baby zucchini attached)

Cut the potato into 1 cm (½ inch) thick pieces. Heat the butter and half the oil in a small saucepan over medium heat. Cook the potato for 15 minutes or until tender. Season with salt and pepper. Set aside and keep warm.

Meanwhile, remove the petals from the zucchini flowers and reserve for garnish. Quarter the remaining zucchini widthways. Heat the remaining oil in a small saucepan. Cook the zucchini for 2 minutes or until tender. Season with salt and pepper. Set aside and keep warm.

PRESENTATION

50 ml (1¾ fl oz) lamb stock (see page 23), warmed
zucchini (courgette) flower petals

Spread the hazelnut purée across 6 plates. Slice each lamb rump into 4 pieces and place on the plate. Place the potato and zucchini alongside and place a pile of parmesan crumbs in between. Finish with a drizzle of lamb stock and garnish with the zucchini flower petals. Serves 6.

DESSERTS

I always enjoy cooking desserts as they allow for greater scope to play with flavours and techniques. I like to feature a savoury edge in my desserts, such as the carrot cake with black olive sorbet (see page 206), in addition to the more traditional sweet suspects. Texture also plays an important part in the experience, making that final mouthful as memorable as it can be. If you want to simplify a dish, make just one or two components.

CHOCOLATE CONE WITH WARM BANANA MILK

CHOCOLATE ICE CREAM

700 ml (24 fl oz) milk

300 ml (10½ fl oz) pouring (single) cream

90 g (3¼ oz) trimoline

75 g (2¾ oz/1⅓ cup) caster (superfine) sugar

300 g (10½ oz) chocolate buttons (53% couverture)

6 g (⅕ oz) stabiliser

Place the milk, cream, trimoline and sugar in a saucepan and bring to the boil, stirring until the sugar is dissolved. Remove from the heat, add the chocolate and stir until melted. Whisk in the stabiliser until combined. Pass through a fine sieve into a metal bowl, then chill over ice. Churn in an ice-cream machine according to the manufacturer's instructions. Transfer to a piping bag fitted with a 2 cm (¾ inch) plain nozzle and place in the freezer for 20 minutes or until set — check on the ice cream regularly, so it doesn't set too hard, or it will be difficult to pipe. If the ice cream becomes too hard, leave it at room temperature until it softens.

This can be made 1 day in advance. Makes 1 litre.

CHOCOLATE CONE

120 g (4¼ oz) store-bought fondant (see Notes)

80 g (2¾ oz) liquid glucose

80 g (2¾ oz) dark chocolate buttons
     (70% couverture), melted

15 g (½ oz) white sesame seeds

15 g (½ oz) black sesame seeds

6 standard metal cone moulds (see Notes)

Preheat the oven to 150°C (300°F/Gas 2).

Place the fondant and glucose in a saucepan and heat to 150°C (300°F). Stir in the chocolate. Working quickly, pour the mixture onto a sheet of baking paper, top with another sheet and, using a rolling pin, roll out to 1 mm (¹⁄₃₂ inch) thick. You may need to place the mixture on a baking tray and warm in the oven to soften, if it gets too hard.

Remove the top sheet of paper and cut into six 10 x 6 cm (4 x 2½ inch) rectangles. Warm in the oven for 2 minutes to soften, then sprinkle evenly with the sesame seeds. Return to the oven for another 2 minutes to soften. Working quickly and with one rectangle at a time, wrap a rectangle around a cone mould. Allow to cool and harden, then remove from the mould. Set aside.

These can be made up to 1 day in advance and stored in an airtight container.

NOTES Cone moulds are available from kitchenware stores. Fondant is available from the baking aisle of supermarkets.

BANANA MILK

3 ripe bananas

250 ml (9 fl oz/1 cup) milk

20 g (⅔ oz) caster (superfine) sugar

2 g (¹⁄₁₆ oz) lecithin, optional (see Note)

Peel and chop the bananas and place in a saucepan. Add the milk, sugar and lecithin, stirring until dissolved. Cover with a cartouche and slowly bring to the boil. Remove from the heat and set aside for 1 hour to infuse. Strain through a fine sieve, discarding the solids. Reheat the milk until warm, then aerate with a stick blender and serve immediately.

NOTE Lecithin is a good addition to liquid mixtures that are aerated because it ensures the air bubbles do not immediately dissipate.

PRESENTATION

Fill the cones with ice cream and serve in an ice-cream holder with a glass of warm banana milk on the side.

SAFFRON-POACHED PEARS WITH BURNT HONEY CREAM AND LIQUID PUFF PASTRY

SAFFRON POACHING LIQUID

125 g (4½ oz) caster (superfine) sugar
150 ml (5 fl oz) Sauternes (see Note)
2 ml (⅟15 fl oz) orange blossom water
1 vanilla bean, split and seeds scraped
20 saffron threads
finely grated zest of 1 orange

Place all the ingredients and 500 ml (17 fl oz/2 cups) water in a saucepan and bring to the boil. Set aside for 20 minutes to infuse.

NOTE Sauternes is a sweet French dessert wine from Bordeaux.

PEAR BALLS AND PEAR PURÉE

6 beurre bosc pears, unpeeled
1 quantity saffron poaching liquid

Using a 1.5 cm (⅝ inch) melon baller (Parisienne cutter), cut out balls from each pear, avoiding the core. You will need 30 balls. Cut the remaining pear into quarters, discarding the cores. Place the balls in the saffron poaching liquid, bring to a simmer and cook for 2–3 minutes or until tender. Using a slotted spoon, remove the balls and set aside to cool.

Add the pear off-cuts to the liquid and cook for 15 minutes or until very tender. Strain, reserving the liquid and pear. Transfer the pear to a blender and blend until smooth, adding a little of the reserved liquid to thin, if necessary. Pass through a fine sieve. Place in a piping bag fitted with a 5 mm (¼ inch) plain nozzle and set aside.

These can be made 1 day in advance and refrigerated.

HONEY JELLY

2 sheets gelatine, titanium strength
100 g (3½ oz) honey

Line the base and sides of a 30 x 20 x 3 cm (12 x 8 x 1¼ inch) tray with freezer film.

Soak the gelatine in cold water for 5 minutes or until softened.

Place the honey in a saucepan, bring to the boil and cook for 1 minute or until caramelised. Add 120 ml (4 fl oz) cold water, then remove from the heat. Squeeze out the excess water from the gelatine, add the gelatine to the honey and stir until dissolved. Pour into the lined tray and refrigerate for 2 hours or until set.

This can be made 1 day in advance.

BURNT HONEY CREAM

85 g (3 oz) honey
1 egg
1 egg yolk
1½ sheets gelatine, titanium strength
50 ml (1¾ fl oz) milk, warmed
300 ml (10½ fl oz) pouring (single) cream, whipped to soft peaks

Place the honey in a small saucepan over medium heat and cook for 1 minute or until caramelised. Remove from the heat and allow to cool for 30 seconds.

Place the egg and egg yolk in a bowl and, using an electric beater, whisk until thick and pale. While whisking continuously, add the hot honey and whisk for about 10 minutes or until thick and pale.

Soak the gelatine in cold water for 5 minutes or until softened, then squeeze out the excess water and dissolve in the warm milk. Gently fold into the honey mixture, then fold in the cream. Spread evenly over the honey jelly. Refrigerate for 2 hours or until set.

LIQUID PUFF PASTRY

40 g (1 ½ oz/⅓ cup) icing (confectioner's) sugar
1 sheet store-bought frozen butter puff pastry, thawed
sea salt flakes
60 ml (2 fl oz/¼ cup) olive oil

Preheat the oven to 170°C (325°F/Gas 3). Sprinkle half of the icing sugar on a baking tray lined with baking paper and top with the puff pastry. Sprinkle over the remaining icing sugar, cover with baking paper, then place another baking tray on top to weight down the pastry and prevent it from rising. Bake for 20 minutes or until the pastry is crisp and the sugar is caramelised. Transfer the pastry to a wire rack to cool.

Break 200 g (7 oz) of the pastry into small pieces and place in a blender. Add a pinch of salt and, with the motor running, gradually add the oil and blend until a fine paste forms. Pour into a 30 x 20 cm (12 x 8 inch) tray lined with freezer film and spread to 4 mm (⅛ inch) thick. Refrigerate for 20 minutes or until set.

TO ASSEMBLE

Place the liquid puff pastry on top of the burnt honey cream and honey jelly in the tray. Gently press down to stick together. Refrigerate for 1 hour or freeze for 30 minutes or until set. Remove from the fridge, invert onto a board and, using a hot knife, cut into 6 equal portions. Refrigerate until ready to serve.

PRESENTATION

Place the burnt honey cream and liquid puff pastry onto 6 plates. Pipe large dots of pear purée next to it and arrange 5 pear balls in between. Serves 6.

TOAST CUSTARD WITH CHOCOLATE PARFAIT AND LYCHEE PURÉE

LYCHEE PURÉE

300 g (10½ oz) peeled and seeded fresh lychees

70 ml (2⅔ fl oz) sugar syrup (see page 25)

2.5 g (¹⁄₁₂ oz) agar agar

Place the lychees and sugar syrup in an upright blender and blend until smooth. Set aside 100 ml (3½ fl oz) for the lychee glass.

Transfer the remaining lychee liquid to a saucepan, add the agar agar, bring to the boil and cook for 2 minutes. Transfer to a metal bowl and chill over ice until firmly set. Return to the blender and blend until smooth. Set aside.

This can be made 1 day in advance and stored in the fridge in an airtight container.

LYCHEE GLASS

100 ml (3½ fl oz) lychee liquid (reserved from lychee purée)

25 g (⅘ oz) isomalt

30 g (1 oz) maltodextrin

Place all the ingredients in a small saucepan and, using a stick blender, blend until combined. Place over medium heat and heat until 80°C (176°F). Spread evenly over a 30 x 20 cm (12 x 8 inch) tray lined with baking paper. Dry in a dehydrator at 80°C (176°F) for 4 hours. Alternatively, place in the oven on the lowest temperature and leave until completely dry. Remove and allow to cool on the tray. Break into small shards.

This can be made 1 day in advance and stored in an airtight container in a dry place.

TOAST CUSTARD

400 g (14 oz) sourdough bread, crusts on

700 ml (24 fl oz) milk

3 sheets gelatine, titanium strength

110 g (3¾ oz/½ cup) caster (superfine) sugar

5 egg yolks

2 egg whites

Preheat the oven to 140°C (275°F/Gas 1). Line the base and sides of a 15 x 10 x 3 cm (6 x 4 x 1¼ inch) baking tray with baking paper.

Slice the bread into 2 cm (¾ inch) thick slices and bake for 10 minutes or until completely dried out, then toast under a hot grill (broiler) until burnt with black edges and dark brown colouring. Place in a saucepan with the milk and bring to the boil, then set aside for 20 minutes to infuse.

Soak the gelatine in cold water for 5 minutes or until softened. Strain the milk, discarding the solids. Return the milk to a clean pan over low heat. Squeeze out the excess water from the gelatine and add the gelatine to the pan, stirring until dissolved.

Place the sugar, egg yolks and egg white in a bowl and whisk until thick and pale. Add the infused milk and whisk to combine. Pour into the lined tray, cover with foil and bake for 20 minutes or until set. Remove from the oven and refrigerate until chilled. Turn out the custard and break into large squares. Refrigerate until ready to serve.

This can be made 1 day in advance and stored in an airtight container.

CHOCOLATE PARFAIT

75 g (2¾ oz) egg yolk (about 6 eggs)
80 g (2¾ oz) caster (superfine) sugar
1½ sheets gelatine, titanium strength
30 g (1 oz) liquid glucose
100 g (3½ oz) dark chocolate buttons (70% couverture)
30 g (1 oz) cocoa
500 ml (17 fl oz/2 cups) pouring (single) cream, whipped to soft peaks

Line the base and sides of a 15 x 10 x 3 cm (6 x 4 x 1¼ inch) tray with plastic wrap.

Using an electric beater, beat the egg yolks and sugar until thick and pale. Soak the gelatine in cold water for 5 minutes or until softened, then squeeze out the excess water. Place the gelatine, glucose, chocolate and cocoa in a double boiler over simmering water and stir until dissolved. Add to the egg yolk mixture, cool to room temperature, then fold in the cream. Transfer to the lined tray and freeze. Remove the parfait from the tray and break into the same-sized pieces as the custard. Return to the freezer until ready to serve.

This can be made 1 day in advance and stored in an airtight container.

COCOA CRUMBS

70 g (2⅔ oz) unsalted butter, softened
45 g (1⅔ oz) caster (superfine) sugar
25 g (⅘ oz) egg white (about 1 egg)
100 g (3½ oz) cocoa, sifted

Preheat the oven to 170°C (325°F/Gas 3). Place the butter and sugar in the bowl of an electric mixer and beat until thick and pale. Add the egg white and beat for 2 minutes, then fold in the cocoa. Spread evenly over a 30 x 20 cm (12 x 8 inch) tray lined with baking paper to 5 mm (¼ inch) thick. Bake for 12 minutes or until evenly coloured. Remove and cool on the tray. Roughly chop and set aside.

This can be made 1 day in advance and stored in an airtight container in the fridge. Bring to room temperature before serving.

PRESENTATION

baby basil leaves, for garnish

Spoon the purée onto 6 plates and sprinkle over the cocoa crumbs. Place the toast custard and chocolate parfait alternately on top of the crumbs. Insert shards of lychee glass in between and garnish with the baby basil. Serves 6.

The cake in this recipe is inspired by the '30-second sponge cake', from Albert Adrià's book *Natura*. I like this recipe because of its innovative cooking technique and it allows me to deliver a freshly baked cake within minutes at the reastaurant.

PISTACHIO CAKE, YOGHURT CREAM AND MANDARIN ICE CREAM

MANDARIN ICE CREAM

400 ml (14 fl oz) pouring (single) cream
10 egg yolks
200 g (7 oz) caster (superfine) sugar
700 ml (24 fl oz) freshly squeezed mandarin juice (about 12 mandarins)

Place the cream in a small saucepan and bring to the boil.

Place the egg yolks and sugar in the bowl of an electric mixer and whisk until thick and pale. While whisking continuously, gradually add the hot cream and whisk until combined. Add the juice and whisk until combined. Chill over ice and pass through a fine sieve. Churn in an ice-cream machine according to the manufacturer's instructions. Freeze until required. Makes 1 litre (35 fl oz/4 cups).

YOGHURT CREAM

1 length 1.5 cm (⅝ inch) diameter PVC piping
1 sheet acetate
2 sheets gelatine, titanium strength
200 ml (7 fl oz) milk
150 ml (5 fl oz) pouring (single) cream
110 g (3¾ oz/½ cup) caster (superfine) sugar
finely grated zest of ½ lemon
250 g (9 oz/1 cup) Greek yoghurt

Cut the PVC piping into six 10 cm (4 inch) long pieces. Cut the acetate into six 12 x 5 cm (4½ x 2 inch) rectangles. Roll each piece widthways, then place each roll inside a piece of PVC pipe. Make sure one end of the acetate sits flush with the pipe and the other end protrudes. Place plastic wrap over the flush end and secure with tape. Stand, covered-end down, on a tray.

Soak the gelatine in water for 5 minutes or until softened. Heat the milk, cream, sugar and zest in a saucepan over low heat, stirring until the sugar is dissolved. Squeeze out the excess water from the gelatine and add the gelatine to the pan, stirring until dissolved. Remove from the heat and gradually whisk in the yoghurt. Pass through a fine sieve. Pour into the moulds and refrigerate for 3 hours or until set.

These can be made 1 day in advance and stored in the moulds in an airtight container in the fridge.

MANDARIN OIL

3 mandarins
30 ml (1 fl oz) olive oil

Using a microplane grater, finely grate the zest of the mandarins into a bowl, making sure you catch all the oils. Discard the mandarins. Transfer the zest to an airtight container, making sure to scrape up the oils. Cover with the olive oil and leave in a warm place for 1 hour to infuse. Strain through a fine sieve, pressing as much oil out of the zest as possible. Discard the zest and set the mandarin oil aside.

MANDARIN POWDER

25 ml (⅘ fl oz) mandarin oil, approximately
15 g (½ oz) maltodextrin
4 g (⅐ oz) icing (confectioner's) sugar
sea salt flakes

Place all the ingredients in a bowl and, using a spoon, rub the ingredients together to form a fine powder. Add extra mandarin oil, if necessary. Set aside.

CRUSHED PISTACHIO

200 g (7 oz/1½ cups) Iranian pistachio kernels
10 g (⅓ oz) sea salt flakes

Crush the pistachios and salt using a mortar and pestle. Set aside.

PISTACHIO CAKE

115 g (4 oz) Iranian pistachio kernels
210 g (7½ oz) egg white (about 7 eggs)
80 g (2¾ oz) egg yolk (about 5 eggs)
170 g (6 oz) caster (superfine) sugar
40 g (1½ oz) plain (all-purpose) flour
20 ml (¾ fl oz) hazelnut liqueur (such as Frangelico)

Place the pistachios, egg white and egg yolk in an upright blender and blend until smooth. Add the sugar, flour and liqueur and blend until combined. Pour into a cream canister and charge twice. Set aside for 1 hour. Fill six plastic drinking cups one-third full with the mixture. Microwave on high for 30 seconds. Cool, then tear each cake into 3. Set aside.

PRESENTATION

To remove the yoghurt creams, remove the plastic wrap and tape, then use the protruding acetate to pull them out of the moulds — the acetate will naturally uncurl. Use the acetate to transfer the creams onto plates. Sprinkle the crushed pistachio in a line around the creams, then sprinkle the mandarin powder on top. Using 2 tablespoons, place a quenelle of ice cream on top of the crushed pistachio and place 3 pieces of cake around. Serves 6.

HOT RICOTTA DUMPLINGS

STRAWBERRY PURÉE

300 g (10½ oz/2 cups) strawberries, hulled
70 ml (2¼ fl oz) sugar syrup (see page 25)
2.5 g (¹⁄₁₂ oz) agar agar

Place the strawberries and sugar syrup in an upright blender and blend until smooth. Pour into a saucepan over medium heat, add the agar agar, bring to the boil and cook for 2 minutes. Transfer to a metal bowl and chill over ice until firmly set. Return to the blender and blend until smooth. Set aside.

CINNAMON SUGAR

75 g (2¾ oz/⅓ cup) caster (superfine) sugar
45 g (1⅔ oz) ground cinnamon

Combine the sugar and cinnamon in a shallow bowl and set aside.

RICOTTA DUMPLINGS

80 g (2¾ oz) plain (all-purpose) flour
2.5 g (¹⁄₁₂ oz) baking powder
finely grated zest of 2 oranges
2 eggs, lightly beaten
1 egg yolk
500 g (1 lb 2 oz/2 cups) firm ricotta, well drained
vegetable oil, for deep-frying
1 quantity cinnamon sugar
1 quantity strawberry purée

Sift the flour and baking powder into a bowl. Add the orange zest, egg and egg yolk and, using an electric beater, beat until combined and smooth. Gradually add the ricotta and beat until smooth. Transfer to a piping bag fitted with a 2 cm (¾ inch) plain nozzle.

Heat the oil in a large deep saucepan or deep-fryer to 180°C (350°F). Pipe small balls about the size of walnuts, in batches of about 8 at a time, into the oil and deep-fry for 2–3 minutes or until golden all over. Remove using tongs, drain on paper towel and, while still hot, roll in the cinnamon sugar. Serve immediately with the strawberry purée. Serves 6 / makes 24.

LIQUID PINEAPPLE WITH SOFT CHOCOLATE AND PINEAPPLE SORBET

PINEAPPLE SORBET

500 g (1 lb 2 oz) peeled, cored and diced Bethonga pineapple (about 1 kg/2 lb 4 oz whole)
juice of 1 lime, or to taste
100 g (3½ oz) caster (superfine) sugar, or to taste
100 g (3½ oz) liquid glucose

Place the pineapple, lime juice, sugar and glucose in an upright blender and blend until smooth. Depending on the sweetness of the pineapple, you may need to add more sugar or lime juice to taste. Pass through a fine sieve. Churn in an ice-cream machine according to the manufacturer's instructions. Freeze until required. Makes 700 ml (24 fl oz).

CHOCOLATE GEL

250 g (9 oz) chocolate buttons (53% couverture)
265 g (9⅓ oz) pouring (single) cream
60 g (2¼ oz) caster (superfine) sugar
1.4 g (¹⁄₂₀ oz) guar gum
2.2 g (¹⁄₁₃ oz) iota
1 g (¹⁄₃₂ oz) kappa

Place the chocolate in a heatproof bowl. Place the cream in a small saucepan and bring to the boil, then pour over the chocolate and stir until smooth.

Place the remaining ingredients and 300 ml (10½ fl oz) water in a small saucepan and, using a stick blender, blend until smooth. Bring to the boil, stirring continuously, then remove from the heat and pour over the chocolate mixture. Working quickly, to avoid the mixture becoming too hard, stir well to combine, then pass through a fine sieve into a 30 x 20 cm (12 x 8 inch) tray lined with plastic wrap. Refrigerate for 1 hour or until set.

This can be made 1 day in advance. When ready to serve, cut lengthways into 5 mm (¼ inch) thick slices. You will need 6 slices.

LICORICE GEL

150 g (5½ oz) good-quality soft licorice, thinly sliced
120 g (4¼ oz) caster (superfine) sugar

Combine the licorice, sugar and 150 ml (5 fl oz) water in a small saucepan over very low heat and cook, stirring occasionally, until the licorice is dissolved and the mixture is smooth, adding a little more water, if necessary. Working quickly, transfer to an upright blender and blend until smooth. While still hot, pass through a fine sieve. Place in a container and store at room temperature.

This can be made 1 day in advance.

LICORICE CRUMBS

250 g (9 oz/2½ cups) ground almonds (almond meal)
160 g (5⅔ oz) licorice gel
150 g (5½ oz) caster (superfine) sugar
150 g (5½ oz/1 cup) plain (all-purpose) flour
110 g (3¾ oz) cocoa
25 g (⅘ oz) ground star anise
100 g (3½ oz) unsalted butter, melted and cooled

Preheat the oven to 80°C (176°F).

Place all the ingredients, except the butter, in a food processor and pulse to combine. With the motor running, pour in the butter and process until large crumbs form. Scatter over a baking tray and dry in the oven for about 30 minutes or until almost dry — the crumbs should separate but still be a little moist. Set aside.

PINEAPPLE GEL

600 g (1 lb 5 oz) peeled, cored and diced Bethonga
    pineapple (about 1.2 kg/2 lb 10 oz)
juice of 1 lime
40 g (1½ oz) caster (superfine) sugar
¼ vanilla bean, split and seeds scraped
2.5 g (¹⁄₁₂ oz) guar gum
4.2 g (³⁄₂₀ oz) iota

Place the pineapple, lime juice, sugar and vanilla seeds in an upright blender and blend until smooth. Pass through a fine sieve placed over a saucepan. Add the guar gum and iota to the pan and, using a stick blender, blend until smooth.

Bring to the boil, stirring continuously, and allow to boil for 30 seconds, then pass through a fine sieve into a 15 x 10 cm (6 x 4 inch) tray lined with plastic wrap. Refrigerate for 2 hours or until set.

This can be made 1 day in advance. When ready to serve, cut into small rectangles. You will need 18 rectangles.

PINEAPPLE SOUP

700 g (1 lb 9 oz) peeled, cored and diced Bethonga
    pineapple (about 1.4 kg/3 lb 2 oz)
25 g (⅘ oz) palm sugar (jaggery), crushed
10 g (⅓ oz) unsalted butter
1 g (¹⁄₃₂ oz) combined freshly ground white
    and Sichuan pepper
½ vanilla bean, split and seeds scraped
1 g (¹⁄₃₂ oz) xanthan gum

Heat a heavy-based saucepan over medium heat. Add the pineapple and cook for 2–3 minutes or until caramelised, then turn over and cook for 1 minute. Add the palm sugar, butter and pepper and cook for 3 minutes or until the pineapple is softened. Transfer to an upright blender, add the vanilla seeds and xanthan gum and blend until smooth. Pass through a fine sieve. Refrigerate until chilled.

This can be made 1 day in advance and stored in an airtight container.

CHOCOLATE TUBES

1 length 3 cm (1¼ inch) diameter PVC piping
2 sheets acetate
200 g (7 oz) dark chocolate buttons (70% couverture)
1 quantity pineapple soup

Cut the PVC piping in six 8 cm (3¼ inch) lengths.

Cut one sheet of acetate into six 11 x 8 cm (4¼ x 3¼ inch) rectangles. Cut the other sheet into six 4 cm (1½ inch) squares.

Melt the chocolate in a double boiler over simmering water. Spread evenly over the acetate rectangles to 1 mm (¹⁄₃₂ inch). Leave at room temperature to cool until almost set. Working with one at a time, and, using the acetate as a guide, curl the chocolate lengthways into a tube and place inside a length of piping, making sure it protrudes from both ends.

To seal one end of the chocolate tubes, spread the melted chocolate evenly over the acetate squares to 1 mm (¹⁄₃₂ inch) thick.Place a square at one end of the chocolate tubes, gently press to seal. Allow to set a little, then carefully peel away the acetate. Trim around the tube with a sharp knife to neaten.

Place in the freezer to quickly set, then fill the tubes with pineapple soup. Repeat the process to seal the other end of the tubes. Refrigerate until ready to serve.

PRESENTATION

Twist the chocolate gel and lay it across the centre of 6 plates. Place 3 piles of licorice crumbs around the gel. Remove the chocolate tubes from the moulds and carefully peel away the acetate. Lay a tube at one end of the chocolate gel. Place 3 rectangles of pineapple gel around the plate. Using 2 tablespoons, place a quenelle of sorbet on top of a pile of licorice crumbs. Dot the licorice gel around the plate to finish. Serves 6.

HONEYCOMB CHOCOLATE BAR

HONEYCOMB

90 g (3¼ oz) caster (superfine) sugar
30 g (1 oz) liquid glucose
5 g (⅙ oz) bicarbonate of soda (baking soda)

Line the base and sides of a 30 x 20 x 3 cm (12 x 8 x 1¼ inch) tray with baking paper.

Place the sugar, glucose and 20 ml (⅔ fl oz) water in a small saucepan and heat to 167°C (333°F), without stirring. Remove from the heat, add the bicarbonate of soda and stir to combine. Pour onto the tray and allow to harden. Break into 2–3 cm (¾–1¼ inch) squares.

CHOCOLATE BAR

600 g (1 lb 5 oz) milk chocolate, chopped
200 ml (7 fl oz) pouring (single) cream
1 quantity honeycomb

Line the base and sides of a 15 x 10 x 4 cm (6 x 4 x 1½ inch) tray with baking paper.

Place the chocolate and cream in a double boiler over simmering water and stir until melted and smooth. Fold in the honeycomb, then pour into the lined tray. Place a sheet of baking paper on top and press down to evenly spread the chocolate. Refrigerate for 2 hours or until set.

COATING

1 quantity chocolate bar
150 g (5½ oz) chocolate buttons (53% couverture)
100 g (3½ oz) cocoa butter (see Note)

Remove the chocolate bar from the fridge and remove from the tray. Cut into six 10 x 2.5 cm (4 x 1 inch) bars. Place the chocolate and cocoa butter in a double boiler over simmering water and stir until melted and smooth. While warm, fill an airbrush (see Note) with the chocolate mixture and spray the chocolate all over the bars to coat evenly. Refrigerate for 15 minutes or until set.

NOTE Cocoa butter is available from gourmet food stores. An airbrush is usually used to apply paint but it is used here to create a thin, textured coating. You can buy it from hardware stores. Ensure it is new or has only ever been used for cooking purposes.

PRESENTATION

sea salt flakes, for garnish

Sprinkle each chocolate bar with salt to serve. Makes 6.

CARROT CAKE WITH
BLACK OLIVE SORBET

BLACK OLIVE SORBET

500 g (1 lb 2 oz/3¼ cups) pitted black Kalamata olives
100 g (3½ oz) liquid glucose
225 g (8 oz) trimoline

Rinse the olives in water and place in a saucepan. Cover with fresh water and bring to the boil. Drain well and repeat blanching and draining twice more.

Gently heat the glucose and trimoline in a small saucepan over low heat until melted. Transfer to a blender, add the olives and 400 ml (14 fl oz) water and blend until smooth. Pass through a fine sieve.

Transfer to a Pacojet container, cover and place in the freezer until frozen, then churn in the Pacojet until a sorbet forms. Place in the freezer until ready to serve. Alternatively, you can churn in an ice-cream machine according to the manufacturer's instructions — do not freeze the mixture before churning.

This can be made 1 day in advance. Makes 700 ml (24 fl oz).

ORANGE BLOSSOM GEL

1¼ sheets gelatine, titanium strength
100 ml (3½ fl oz) sugar syrup (see page 25)
15 ml (½ fl oz) orange blossom water

Soak the gelatine in cold water for 5 minutes or until softened, then squeeze out the excess water and place the gelatine in a saucepan with the sugar syrup, orange blossom water and 135 ml (4½ fl oz) water over medium heat and stir until the gelatine is dissolved. Pass through a fine sieve. Transfer to a container and refrigerate for 1 hour or until set.

COFFEE AND PISTACHIO CRUMBS

125 g (4½ oz) Iranian pistachio kernels
15 g (½ oz) instant coffee granules
100 g (3½ oz) caster (superfine) sugar
100 g (3½ oz) unsalted butter, diced
75 g (2¾ oz/½ cup) plain (all-purpose) flour

Place the pistachios, coffee granules and sugar in a food processor and process until ground. Add the butter and flour and pulse until just combined. Roll out thinly between baking paper to form a 30 x 20 cm (12 x 8 inch) rectangle. Place on a baking tray and rest in the fridge for at least 30 minutes.

Preheat the oven to 160°C (315°F/Gas 2–3). Remove the top sheet of baking paper and bake for 12 minutes or until golden. Remove from the oven and allow to cool on the tray. Using a mortar and pestle, crush the coffee and pistachio biscuit into fine crumbs.

CARROT PURÉE

2 litres (70 fl oz) freshly juiced carrot juice (about 5 kg/11 lb 4 oz carrots)
17.5 g (⅔ oz) agar agar
70 ml (2¼ fl oz) vegetable oil

Place the juice in a large saucepan and bring to a rapid boil, then remove immediately from the heat. Set aside 200 ml (7 fl oz) of the juice. Return the pan to medium heat and cook, stirring occasionally, for 30 minutes or until reduced to 700 ml (24 fl oz).

Add the agar agar and bring to the boil. Remove from the heat and cool to room temperature. Refrigerate for 1 hour or until set. Transfer to a blender, add the oil and just enough of the reserved juice to make a smooth paste, then blend until combined. Pass through a fine sieve. Set aside.

CARROT CAKE

3 eggs
200 g (7 oz) caster (superfine) sugar
300 g (10½ oz) carrot purée
30 ml (1 fl oz) olive oil
180 g (6½ oz) plain (all-purpose) flour
10 g (⅓ oz) baking powder

Preheat the oven to 180°C (350°F/Gas 4). Lightly grease and line a 30 x 20 cm (12 x 8 inch) cake tin. Place the eggs and sugar in a large bowl and, using an electric beater, beat until thick and pale. Add the carrot purée and oil and beat to combine. Sift over the flour and baking powder and mix thoroughly. Pour into the lined tin and bake for 1 hour or until an inserted skewer comes out clean. Remove from the tin and cool on a wire rack. Cut the cake into six 10 x 4 cm (4 x 1½ inch) portions. Set aside.

PRESENTATION

Halve each carrot cake portion widthways. Place one standing and the other piece lying down on 6 plates. Place some purée alongside a piece of cake. Place a small spoonful of crumbs next to each piece. Using a warm teaspoon, scoop some gel on top of both piles of crumbs. Using 2 tablespoons, place a quenelle of sorbet on top of a piece of cake. Serves 6.

TONKA BEAN ICE CREAM WITH CHOCOLATE AND CHESTNUT CAKE

TONKA BEAN ICE CREAM

300 ml (10½ fl oz) milk
300 ml (10½ fl oz) pouring (single) cream
3 tonka beans, finely grated
sea salt flakes
5 egg yolks
110 g (3¾ oz/½ cup) caster (superfine) sugar
40 g (1½ oz) stabiliser

Place the milk, cream, tonka bean and a pinch of salt in a saucepan and bring to the boil.

Place the egg yolks, sugar and stabiliser in the bowl of an electric mixer and whisk until light and pale. While whisking, gradually add the milk mixture and whisk until well combined. Chill over ice. Pass through a fine sieve. Churn in an ice-cream machine according to the manufacturer's instructions. Freeze until required. Makes 1 litre (35 fl oz/4 cups).

FROZEN CHOCOLATE POWDER

50 g (1¾ oz) chocolate buttons (53% couverture)
30 g (1 oz/¼ cup) cocoa
30 g (1 oz) caster (superfine) sugar
100 ml (3½ fl oz) pouring (single) cream

Place the chocolate, cocoa, sugar, cream and 150 ml (5 fl oz) water in a small saucepan over low heat and stir until the chocolate is melted and the sugar is dissolved. Set aside 60 ml (2 fl oz/¼ cup) chocolate sauce for the presentation.

Pour the remaining chocolate mixture into a 15 x 10 cm (6 x 4 inch) metal container and freeze for 4 hours or until solid.

When ready to serve, use a fork to scrape the frozen mixture to form a fine powder.

CHOCOLATE MOUSSE

1 sheet gelatine, titanium strength
200 g (7 oz) chocolate buttons (53% couverture)
1 teaspoon ground cardamom

Soak the gelatine in cold water for 5 minutes or until softened.

Place the chocolate, cardamom and 500 ml (17 fl oz/2 cups) water in a double boiler over simmering water and stir until melted and smooth. Squeeze out the excess water from the gelatine, add the gelatine to the chocolate mixture and stir until dissolved. Pass through a fine sieve. Place in a cream canister and charge twice. Refrigerate for 1 hour or until set.

CHESTNUT CAKE

2 eggs, separated
60 g (2 oz) honey
30 g (1 oz) caster (superfine) sugar
120 g (4¼ oz) chestnut flour (see Note)
30 g (1 oz/¼ cup) cocoa
¼ teaspoon bicarbonate of soda (baking soda)
¼ teaspoon baking powder
50 ml (1¾ fl oz) extra virgin olive oil

Preheat the oven to 185°C (365°F/Gas 4–5). Line the base and sides of a 15 x 10 x 3 cm (6 x 4 x 1¼ inch) tray with baking paper.

Place the egg yolks, honey and half of the sugar in the bowl of an electric mixer and whisk until the sugar is dissolved and the mixture is thick and pale. Sift together the chestnut flour, cocoa, bicarbonate of soda and baking powder, then stir into the egg mixture.

Place the egg white and remaining sugar in a bowl and whisk together until soft peaks form. Fold one-third into the cake mixture to loosen, then fold in the remainder. Pour into the lined tray and bake for 25 minutes or until an inserted skewer comes out clean. Remove from the oven, turn out and cool on a wire rack.

Using a tall 3 cm (1¼ inch) round cutter, cut out 6 cylinders from the cake. Set aside.

NOTE Chestnut flour is available from health food stores.

CHOCOLATE SPHERES

6 g (⅕ oz) calcium chloride
100 g (3½ oz) chocolate buttons (53% couverture)
25 g (⅘ oz) cocoa
150 ml (5 fl oz) sugar syrup (see page 25)
5 g (⅙ oz) sodium alginate

Combine the calcium chloride with 500 ml (17 fl oz/2 cups) water. Set the calcium bath aside.

Place the chocolate, cocoa, sugar syrup and 300 ml (10½ fl oz) water in a double boiler over simmering water and stir until melted and combined. Remove from the heat and allow to cool to below room temperature.

Transfer the chocolate mixture to an upright blender, add the alginate and blend until smooth.

Transfer to a bowl. Using a round tablespoon measuring spoon, spoon the mixture into the calcium bath, placing no more than 6 balls at a time into the bath. Leave in the bath for approximately 1½ minutes or until a skin forms. Scoop out using a slotted spoon, then rinse in a clean water bath. Scoop out again and drain on paper towel. You will need 6 spheres. Serve immediately.

PRESENTATION

60 ml (2 fl oz/¼ cup) chocolate sauce, warmed
(reserved from frozen chocolate powder)

Spread the chocolate over 6 plates. Pipe the chocolate mousse on top and place a chocolate sphere next to it Using 2 tablespoons, place a quenelle of ice cream on the plate and sprinkle with the chocolate powder. Finish with a piece of chestnut cake on the plate. Serves 6.

POACHED PEACH WITH BLUEBERRIES AND MAGNOLIA ICE CREAM

BLUEBERRY GEL

250 g (9 oz/1⅔ cups) blueberries
60 g (2¼ oz) caster (superfine) sugar
2 sheets gelatine, titanium strength

Place the blueberries and sugar in a heatproof bowl and cover with plastic wrap. Place over a saucepan of simmering water and cook for 40 minutes or until very soft.

Soak the gelatine in water for 5 minutes or until softened. Strain the blueberries through a fine sieve, discarding the solids. Place the liquid in a saucepan over medium heat, squeeze out the excess water from the gelatine and add to the pan, stirring to dissolve. Remove from the heat and spread evenly over a 30 x 20 cm (12 x 8 inch) tray lined with freezer film. Refrigerate for 1 hour or until set. Halve the gel lengthways, then cut each widthways into 3 pieces.

This can be made 1 day in advance and stored in the fridge in an airtight container.

MAGNOLIA ICE CREAM

105 g (3⅔ oz) caster (superfine) sugar
3.5 g (⅛ oz) guar gum
15 g (½ oz) liquid glucose
15 g (½ oz) trimoline
500 ml (17 fl oz/2 cups) milk
30 g (1 oz) powdered milk
130 ml (4¼ fl oz) pouring (single) cream
20 ml (⅔ fl oz) magnolia essence (see Note)

Place the sugar, guar gum, glucose and trimoline in a saucepan and bring to the boil. Stir in the remaining ingredients, then remove from the heat, transfer to a metal bowl and chill over ice. Churn in an ice-cream machine. Freeze until required. Makes 1 litre (35 fl oz/4 cups).

NOTE It's important to use food-grade magnolia essence, available from aromatherapy stores.

POACHED PEACH

200 g (7 oz) caster (superfine) sugar
6 ripe but firm freestone (slipstone) peaches

Place the sugar in a saucepan with 400 ml (14 fl oz) water and bring to the boil. Add the peaches, then remove from the heat and cool in the liquid. Remove the peaches from the liquid, peel and quarter. Discard the liquid. Set aside.

BLUEBERRIES

50 ml (1¾ fl oz) sugar syrup (see page 25)
200 g (7 oz/1⅓ cups) blueberries

Place the sugar syrup and one-quarter of the blueberries in a saucepan and bring to the boil. Remove from the heat, then crush to form a thick compote. Cool, then stir through the remaining blueberries. Set aside.

BLACK PASTRY CRUMBS

125 g (4½ oz) unsalted butter, softened
150 g (5½ oz) caster (superfine) sugar
1 egg
50 g (1¾ oz) hard-boiled egg yolks (about 3 eggs)
250 g (9 oz/1⅔ cups) plain (all-purpose) flour
40 g (1½ oz) ground almonds (almond meal)
2 g (¹⁄₁₆ oz) sea salt flakes
7 g (¼ oz) baking powder
15 g (½ oz) vegetable carbon

Preheat the oven to 160°C (315°F/Gas 2–3). Place the butter and sugar in the bowl of an electric mixer and beat until pale and the sugar is dissolved. Add the egg and beat until combined. Add the egg yolk and beat until smooth. Fold in the remaining ingredients. Turn the dough out and roll between baking paper to 5 mm (¼ inch) thick. Place on a baking tray, remove the top sheet of paper and bake for 15 minutes or until evenly coloured. Cool on the tray, then crush, using a mortar and pestle, into fine crumbs.

PRESENTATION

Arrange the peach on plates and drape a sheet of gel over. Place piles of crumbs around and using 2 tablespoons, place a quenelle of ice cream on one of the piles. Spoon the blueberries around the plate to finish. Serves 6.

RHUBARB CUSTARD AND TUILE
AND VANILLA BEAN ICE CREAM

PISTACHIO PRALINE

100 g (3½ oz) caster (superfine) sugar
100 g (3½ oz/½ cup) Iranian pistachio kernels

Place the sugar and 50 ml (1¾ fl oz) water in a small saucepan, bring to the boil, without stirring, and cook until it reaches 118°C (244°F) and has become a caramel. Remove from the heat and add the pistachios. Pour over a 30 x 20 cm (12 x 8 inch) tray lined with baking paper. Leave to harden and cool to room temperature, then crush, using a mortar and pestle, into fine crumbs.

This can be made 2 days in advance and stored in an airtight container in the freezer.

VANILLA BEAN ICE CREAM

300 ml (10½ fl oz) milk
300 ml (10½ fl oz) pouring (single) cream
2 vanilla beans, split
5 egg yolks
110 g (3¾ oz/½ cup) caster (superfine) sugar
40 g (1½ oz) stabiliser
sea salt flakes

Place the milk, cream and halved vanilla beans in a saucepan and bring to the boil. Remove from the heat and keep warm. Remove the vanilla bean halves.

Place the egg yolks, sugar and stabiliser in the bowl of an electric mixer and whisk until light and pale. While whisking continuously, gradually add the hot milk mixture until well combined. Chill over ice, then pass through a fine sieve. Churn in an ice-cream machine according to the manufacturer's instructions. Freeze until required. Makes 750 ml (26 fl oz/3 cups).

RHUBARB JUICE AND PURÉE

250 g (9 oz) rhubarb
25 g (⅘ oz) caster (superfine) sugar

Preheat the oven to 180°C (350°F/Gas 4). Remove the rhubarb leaves and discard. Cut the stalks into 5 cm (2 inch) lengths, place in a roasting tray with the sugar and 125 ml (4¼ fl oz/½ cup) water, cover with foil and bake for 40 minutes or until collapsed. Pass through a fine sieve, pressing down on the solids to extract as much juice as possible. Set aside the juice to make the rhubarb custard, Turkish delight and rose foam. Transfer the solids to a blender and blend until smooth. Pass through a fine sieve. Set the purée aside.

RHUBARB CUSTARD

1 length 3 cm (1¼ inch) diameter PVC piping
1 sheet acetate
160 ml (5¼ fl oz) rhubarb juice
3 eggs, lightly beaten
25 ml (⅘ fl oz) pouring (single) cream
25 g (⅘ oz) caster (superfine) sugar
1 sheet gelatine, titanium strength

Cut the PVC piping into six 7 cm (2¾ inch) long pieces. Cut the acetate into six 10 x 7 cm (4 x 2¾ inch) rectangles. Roll each piece lengthways, then place inside a piece of PVC pipe. Make sure one end of the acetate sits flush with the pipe and the other end protrudes. Place plastic wrap over the flush end and secure with tape. Stand, covered-end down, on a tray.

Place the juice, eggs, cream and sugar in a Thermomix and cook at 80°C (176°F) for 8 minutes. Alternatively, place in a double boiler over simmering water and whisk continuously for 15 minutes or until thickened and the mixture reaches 80°C — make sure it doesn't overheat or it will split. Soak the gelatine in cold water for 5 minutes or until softened, then squeeze out the excess water and add the gelatine to the rhubarb mixture, stirring until dissolved.

Pass through a fine sieve and spoon into the moulds. Refrigerate for 8 hours or until set.

RHUBARB TUILES

150 g (5½ oz) rhubarb purée
15 g (½ oz) isomalt
10 g (⅓ oz) liquid glucose
1 g (1⁄32 oz) xanthan gum

Preheat the oven to 120°C (235°F/Gas ½).

Place all the ingredients in a Thermomix and cook at 80°C (176°F) for 10 minutes or until thickened. Alternatively, place in a double boiler over simmering water and whisk continuously for 12 minutes or until thickened and the mixture reaches 80°C.

Spread over a non-stick baking mat to form 2 mm (1⁄16 inch) thick, 20 x 2 cm (8 x ¾ inch) rectangles. You will need 6 rectangles. Dry in the oven for 40 minutes or until dry. Working with one tuile at a time and while they're still hot, wrap around a rolling pin to form a twirl, then remove.

These can be made 1 day in advance and stored in an airtight container.

TURKISH DELIGHT

45 ml (1½ fl oz) rhubarb juice
110 g (3¾ oz/½ cup) caster (superfine) sugar
90 g (3¼ oz) liquid glucose
3 sheets gelatine, titanium strength
5 g (⅙ oz) tartaric acid
1 teaspoon rosewater
55 g (2 oz) corn flour (cornstarch)
5 g (⅙ oz) icing (confectioner's) sugar

Reduce the rhubarb juice over medium heat until 20 ml (⅔ fl oz). Place the sugar, glucose and 60 ml (2 fl oz/¼ cup) water in a saucepan and heat to 125°C (257°F).

Meanwhile, soak the gelatine in cold water for 5 minutes or until softened, then squeeze out the excess water and add the gelatine to the pan with the tartaric acid and stir until dissolved. Remove from the heat and cool to 60°C (140°F). Stir in the rosewater and reduced rhubarb juice.

Transfer the liquid to a sauce bottle with a 3 mm (⅛ inch) opening. Place 50 g (1¾ oz) corn flour in a 15 x 10 cm (6 x 4 inch) plastic container. Squeeze small drops (about ½ teaspoon) of liquid into the corn flour to make about 60 drops. Refrigerate for 2 hours or until set.

Sift together the icing sugar and remaining corn flour in a bowl. Tip the drops into a sieve, shaking to remove the excess corn flour, then tip into the icing sugar mixture and toss to coat, shaking off excess.

ROSE FOAM

50 ml (1¾ fl oz) rhubarb juice
30 ml (1 fl oz) rosewater
40 ml (1¼ fl oz) rose syrup (see Note)
1 g (1⁄32 oz) xanthan gum
4 g (⅐ oz) methylcellulose

Place all the ingredients and 700 ml (24 fl oz) water in a bowl and, using a stick blender, blend until combined. Place in the freezer and cool to 1–4°C (34–39°F). Transfer to the bowl of an electric mixer and whisk for 15–20 minutes or until light and foamy. Serve immediately.

This recipe makes more than you will need.

NOTE Rose syrup is available from gourmet food stores or you can make your own: add 1 drop of rosewater to ½ quantity sugar syrup (see page 25).

PRESENTATION

Place the pistachio praline on a plate. To remove the rhubarb custards, remove the plastic wrap and tape, then use the protruding acetate to carefully pull them out of the moulds — the acetate will naturally uncurl from around the custards. Use the acetate to transfer the custards to the praline and roll to coat well. Slice each custard into 3 pieces and plate onto 6 plates. Place a pile of Turkish delight drops on the plates and, using 2 tablespoons, place a quenelle of ice cream on top. Spoon the rose foam around the plate and garnish with a tuile. Serves 6.

CHOCOLATE GANACHE WITH ORANGE OIL, SPICE AND SALT

ORANGE OIL

2 oranges
100 ml (3½ fl oz) extra virgin olive oil

Using a microplane grater, finely grate the zest of the oranges into a bowl, making sure you catch all the oils. Discard the oranges. Transfer the zest to an airtight container, making sure to scrape up the oils. Cover with the olive oil and leave in a warm, room temperature place for 1–2 days to infuse.

CHOCOLATE GANACHE

400 g (14 oz) chocolate buttons (53% couverture)

Bring 350 ml (12 fl oz) water to the boil. Place the chocolate in a heatproof bowl, pour over the boiled water and stir until melted and smooth. Allow to cool to 35°C (95°F). Transfer to the bowl of an electric mixer and whisk until cool and thickened slightly. Refrigerate for 2 hours or until set.

SPICE MIX

25 g (⅘ oz) coriander seeds
15 g (½ oz) black peppercorns
20 g (⅔ oz) cardamom seeds
1 cinnamon stick
1 star anise
7 g (¼ oz) caster (superfine) sugar

Preheat the oven to 170°C (325°F/Gas 3). Roast the spices for 8 minutes, then grind in a spice grinder. Add the sugar and grind until the sugar is powdered. Pass through a fine sieve. Set aside.

PRESENTATION

sea salt flakes, for garnish

Place 20 ml (⅔ fl oz) orange oil in the centre of 6 plates. Using 2 tablespoons, place a quenelle of ganache on top. Finish with some zest from the oil and sprinkle over the spice mix and salt. Serves 6.

CHEESECAKE WITH BEURRE NOISETTE, COFFEE PURÉE, CUMQUAT AND LEMON MERINGUE

PUMPKIN ICE CREAM

300 g (10½ oz) jap pumpkin (winter squash), unpeeled and seeds removed
60 g (2¼ oz) egg yolk (about 4 eggs)
140 g (5 oz) caster (superfine) sugar
380 ml (2½ fl oz) milk
80 ml (2½ fl oz/⅓ cup) pouring (single) cream
10 g (⅓ oz) ground cinnamon

Preheat the oven to 170°C (325°F/Gas 3). Place the pumpkin in a roasting tray and roast for 40 minutes or until tender. Remove from the oven and allow to cool. Remove and discard the skin. Place the flesh in an upright blender and blend until smooth. Set aside.

Place the egg yolk and sugar in the bowl of an electric mixer and whisk until thick and pale.

Place the milk, cream and cinnamon in a saucepan and bring to the boil. Pour over the egg yolk mixture, add the pumpkin purée and stir to combine well. Pass through a fine sieve, then chill over ice. Churn in an ice-cream machine according to the manufacturer's instructions. Freeze until required. Makes 1 litre (35 fl oz/4 cups).

LEMON MERINGUE

115 ml (3¾ fl oz) lemon juice
50 g (1¾ oz) caster (superfine) sugar
10 g (⅓ oz) powdered egg white (see Note)

Place the lemon juice and sugar in a small saucepan and bring to the boil, stirring to dissolve the sugar. Transfer to a metal bowl and chill over ice. Add the powdered egg white and allow to soak for 1 hour.

Preheat the oven to 90°C (194°F). Transfer the mixture to the bowl of an electric mixer and whisk until stiff peaks form. Place in a piping bag fitted with a 1.5 cm (⅝ inch) plain nozzle and pipe teaspoonfuls of meringue onto a baking tray lined with baking paper. Bake for 2–3 hours or until the meringue is crisp.

These can be made 1 day in advance and stored in an airtight container.

NOTE The use of powdered egg white instead of regular egg white makes these meringues lighter and crisper. Powdered egg white is available from health food stores.

CHEESECAKE

375 g (13 oz/1½ cups) ricotta
160 g (5¾ oz/⅔ cup) cream cheese
150 g (5½ oz) crème fraîche
100 g (3½ oz) caster (superfine) sugar
1 vanilla bean, split and seeds scraped
finely grated zest of ½ orange
finely grated zest of ½ lemon
5 sheets gelatine, titanium strength
100 ml (3½ fl oz) pouring (single) cream

Line the base and sides of a 20 x 20 x 5 cm (8 x 8 x 2 inch) tray with freezer film.

Place the ricotta, cream cheese, crème fraîche, sugar, vanilla bean seeds and citrus zest in an upright blender and blend until smooth.

Soak the gelatine in cold water for 5 minutes or until softened, then squeeze out the excess water. Place the gelatine in a small saucepan over medium heat, stirring until dissolved. Add to the blender and blend until combined and smooth. Transfer the mixture to a plastic container and refrigerate for 2 hours or until set.

Remove the cheesecake from the fridge and place in the bowl of an electric mixer. With the motor running on high speed, gradually add the cream and beat for 10 minutes or until light and fluffy. Transfer to the lined tray and refrigerate for 2 hours or until set.

This can be made 1 day in advance. When ready to serve, using a hot sharp knife, cut the cheesecake into 3 cm (1¼ inch) thick strips.

COFFEE PURÉE

125 ml (4¼ fl oz/½ cup) espresso coffee
60 g (2¼ oz) caster (superfine) sugar
3 g (⅒ oz) agar agar

Place the espresso, sugar and 125 ml (4¼ fl oz/½ cup) water in a small saucepan over medium heat and stir until the sugar is dissolved. Add the agar agar, bring to the boil and cook for 1 minute. Transfer to a container and refrigerate for 1 hour or until firmly set. Transfer to an upright blender and blend until smooth. Set aside.

BEURRE NOISETTE

400 g (14 oz) unsalted butter, chopped
200 g (7 oz/2 cups) powdered milk
30 g (1 oz/¼ cup) icing (confectioner's) sugar

Place the butter and powdered milk in a saucepan, bring to the boil and cook, while stirring, for about 5 minutes or until the butter turns brown and the powdered milk is caramelised. Strain the butterfat off, reserving the solids in the pan. Allow the solids to cool, then fold through the icing sugar. Set aside.

CUMQUATS

200 g (7 oz) cumquats, halved and pitted
150 g (5½ oz) caster (superfine) sugar

Place the cumquats in a saucepan, cover with water, bring to the boil, then drain. Repeat blanching and draining twice. Add the sugar and 300 ml (10½ fl oz) water to the pan, place over low heat and simmer for 30 minutes or until the cumquats are candied and translucent. Allow to cool, then drain, discarding the liquid. Set the cumquats aside.

PRESENTATION

Arrange the cheesecake strips on plates in an S shape. Place 3 piles of beurre noisette around the plate. Top 2 of the piles each with a cumquat half and, using 2 tablespoons, place a quenelle of ice cream on the third pile. Dot some coffee purée around the plate, alternating with the meringues. Serves 6.

PASSIONFRUIT MARSHMALLOWS

25 g (⅘ oz) liquid glucose
250 g (9 oz) caster (superfine) sugar
7 sheets gelatine, titanium strength
80 g (2¾ oz) egg white (about 3 eggs)
5 g (⅙ oz) sea salt flakes
250 g (9 oz) passionfruit purée (see Note)
5 g (⅙ oz) citric acid
icing (confectioner's) sugar, for dusting

Place the glucose, sugar and 120 ml (4 fl oz) water in a saucepan and heat to 117°C (243°F).

Soak the gelatine in cold water for 5 minutes or until softened, then squeeze out the excess water. Place the gelatine in a double boiler over simmering water and stir until dissolved.

Meanwhile, place the egg white and salt in the bowl of an electric mixer and whisk until stiff peaks form. While whisking continuously at high speed, add the hot sugar syrup, then the melted gelatine, passionfruit purée and citric acid. Whisk for 15–20 minutes or until cooled. Spread the mixture evenly over a 30 x 20 cm (12 x 8 inch) tray lined with baking paper to about 2.5 cm (1 inch) thick. Refrigerate for 2 hours or until set.

When ready to serve, remove from the fridge and cut into 2.5 cm (1 inch) squares. You can use a blowtorch to toast the marshmallows, if desired.

NOTE I prefer to use Boiron frozen fruit purées for their intense flavour.

MALTED MILK MARSHMALLOWS

40 g (1½ oz) liquid glucose
100 g (3½ oz) caster (superfine) sugar
3½ sheets gelatine, titanium strength
75 g (2¾ oz) egg white (about 3 eggs)
70 g (2⅔ oz) powdered milk
25 ml (⅘ fl oz) milk
25 g (⅘ oz) malt powder

Place the glucose, sugar and 50 ml (1¾ fl oz) of water in a saucepan and heat to 117°C (243°F).

Soak the gelatine in cold water for 5 minutes or until softened, then squeeze out the excess water. Place the gelatine in a double boiler over simmering water and stir until dissolved.

Meanwhile, place the egg white and powdered milk in the bowl of an electric mixer and whisk until stiff peaks form. While whisking continuously at high speed, add the hot sugar syrup, then the melted gelatine and whisk for 15–20 minutes or until cooled. Lay a 50 x 40 cm (20 x 16 inch) double layer of plastic wrap on a work surface. Using a spatula, spread the mixture evenly over the plastic wrap, leaving a 10 cm (4 inch) border on each side. Using the plastic wrap as a guide, roll the marshmallow up lengthways into a cylinder. Tie the ends tightly to secure and refrigerate for 1–2 hours or until set.

Remove from the fridge and remove the plastic wrap. Cut into 2.5 cm (1 inch) long pieces.

When ready to serve, use a blowtorch to toast the marshmallows, then sprinkle with the malt powder.

STRAWBERRY MARSHMALLOWS

10 g (⅓ oz) liquid glucose
225 g (8 oz) caster (superfine) sugar
3½ sheets gelatine, titanium strength
80 g (2¾ oz) egg white (about 3 eggs)
75 g (2¾ oz) strawberry purée (see Note, left)
1½ teaspoons lemon juice
25 ml (⅘ fl oz) strawberry liqueur
icing (confectioner's) sugar, for dusting

Place the glucose, sugar and 120 ml (4 fl oz) water in a saucepan and heat to 117°C (243°F).

Soak the gelatine in cold water for 5 minutes or until softened, then squeeze out the excess water. Place the gelatine in a double boiler over simmering water and stir until dissolved.

Meanwhile, place the egg white in the bowl of an electric mixer and whisk until stiff peaks form. While whisking continuously at high speed, add the hot sugar syrup, then the melted gelatine, strawberry purée, lemon juice and strawberry liqueur and whisk for 15–20 minutes or until cooled. Spread the mixture evenly over a 30 x 20 cm (12 x 8 inch) tray lined with baking paper to about 2.5 cm (1 inch) thick. Refrigerate for 2 hours or until set.

When ready to serve, remove from the fridge, cut into 2.5 cm (1 inch) squares and dust with icing sugar.

COCONUT MOUSSE WITH CHERRY SORBET AND CHOCOLATE CRUMBS

COCONUT POWDER

50 g (1¾ oz) desiccated coconut
40 g (1½ oz/⅓ cup) icing (confectioner's) sugar
30 g (1 oz) maltodextrin

Place all the ingredients in a food processor and pulse into a fine powder.
This can be made 3 days in advance and stored in an airtight container.

COCONUT MOUSSE

4½ sheets gelatine, titanium strength
150 ml (5 fl oz) fresh young coconut juice
150 ml (5 fl oz) Kara coconut cream
200 ml (7 fl oz) sugar syrup (see page 25)

Soak the gelatine in cold water for 5 minutes or until softened.
Place the coconut juice in a saucepan and bring to the boil. Squeeze out the excess water
from the gelatine and add the gelatine to the pan, stirring until dissolved. Add the coconut
cream and sugar syrup and stir until combined. Remove from the heat, pour into a plastic
15 x 10 cm (6 x 4 inch) container and refrigerate for 2 hours or until firmly set.
Place the mixture in the bowl of an electric mixer and whisk on medium–high speed
for 10 minutes or until doubled in volume. Transfer to a piping bag fitted with a 1 cm
(½ inch) plain nozzle and refrigerate until ready to serve.
This can be made 1 day in advance.

CHERRY GEL

1½ sheets gelatine, titanium strenth
200 ml (7 fl oz) cherry purée (see Note, page 231)
50 g (1¾ oz) caster (superfine) sugar

Soak the gelatine in cold water for 5 minutes or until softened.
Place the cherry purée and sugar in a saucepan over medium heat and stir until the
sugar is dissolved. Squeeze the excess water from the gelatine and add the gelatine to
the pan, stirring until dissolved. Remove from the heat, pour into a plastic 15 x 10 cm
(6 x 4 inch) container and refrigerate for 2 hours or until firmly set.
Remove the gel from the container and, using a sharp knife, cut it into 1 cm (½ inch)
cubes. Refrigerate until ready to serve.
This can be made up to 2 days in advance and stored in an airtight container.

CHERRY SORBET

400 ml (14 fl oz) cherry purée (see Note)
50 g (1¾ oz) trimoline
40 g (1½ oz) liquid glucose

Place half of the cherry purée in a saucepan over medium heat. Add the trimoline and glucose and stir until well combined.

Place the remaining purée in a heatproof bowl. Add the hot cherry mixture and stir until combined.

Transfer to a Pacojet container, cover and place in the freezer until frozen, then churn in the Pacojet until a sorbet forms. Place in the freezer until ready to serve. Alternatively, you can churn it in an ice-cream machine according to the manufacturer's instructions — do not freeze mixture before churning.

This can be made 1 day in advance. Makes 500 ml (17 fl oz/2 cups).

NOTE I prefer to use Boiron frozen cherry purée for its intense flavour.

CHOCOLATE-CHERRY CRUMBS

150 g (5½ oz) unsalted butter, chopped and softened
150 g (5½ oz) caster (superfine) sugar
1 egg
200 g (7 oz/1⅓ cups) plain (all-purpose) flour
70 g (2⅔ oz/½ cup) cocoa
60 g (2¼ oz) ground almonds (almond meal)

Preheat the oven to 160°C (315°F/Gas 2–3).

Place the butter and sugar in the bowl of an electric mixer and beat on medium speed until pale and the sugar is dissolved. Add the egg and beat until combined. Fold through the flour, cocoa and ground almonds. Spread evenly over a 40 x 30 cm (16 x 12 inch) baking tray lined with baking paper. Place another sheet of baking paper on top and bake for 20 minutes or until evenly coloured. Remove and cool on the tray. Using a mortar and pestle, crush into coarse crumbs.

This can be made 1 day in advance and should be stored in an airtight container.

PRESENTATION

12 cherries, pitted and halved

Pipe the coconut mousse in a mound onto 6 plates and sprinkle over the crumbs to completely cover. Sprinkle the coconut powder over the crumbs. Arrange 5 cubes of cherry gel and 4 cherry halves in the crumbs. Using 2 tablespoons, place a quenelle of sorbet alongside the crumbs. Serves 6.

DRINKS

These cocktails are out-of-the-ordinary drinks with a bit of an edge. They are very simple to reproduce at home as most are a twist on a classic. The use of premium ingredients and spirits is paramount and will really make these cocktails shine. These drinks are not too fruity or sweet, so you can enjoy them at any stage of your meal. Wine plays an important part in rounding out a dish. Nick Hildebrandt shares his philosophy for food and wine pairing with some of his favourite matches.

FROZEN 'POPCORN' HEMINGWAY

3½ sheets gelatine, titanium strength
210 ml (7½ fl oz) white rum
150 ml (5 fl oz) freshly squeezed pink grapefruit juice (about 1 grapefruit)
120 ml (4 fl oz/½ cup) lime juice
45 ml (1½ fl oz) maraschino cherry liqueur
180 ml (5¾ fl oz) sugar syrup (see page 25)
600 ml (21 fl oz) liquid nitrogen
finely grated lime zest, for garnish

Soak the gelatine in cold water for 5 minutes or until softened.

Place the rum, grapefruit juice, lime juice, maraschino liqueur and sugar syrup in a bowl and stir to combine. Transfer 100 ml (3½ fl oz) to a saucepan over medium heat. Squeeze out the excess water from the gelatine and add the gelatine to the pan, stirring until dissolved. Allow to cool, then combine with the remaining rum mixture.

Pour into a cream canister and charge twice. Discharge 150 ml (5 fl oz) of the rum mixture into a stainless steel bowl. Add 100 ml (3½ fl oz) liquid nitrogen and, using a spatula, stir and break into popcorn-sized pieces. Place in a martini glass, scatter over the lime zest and serve immediatley with a teaspoon. Repeat with the remaining rum mixture. Serves 6.

MR PINK

20 ml (⅔ fl oz) Campari
20 ml (⅔ fl oz) elderflower liqueur (such as St-Germain)
60 ml (2 fl oz/¼ cup) fiano vermouth
juice of ½ lemon
orange slice, for garnish

Place all the ingredients, except the orange slice, in a boston glass. Stir to combine, then strain into an old-fashioned tumbler filled with ice cubes. Garnish with the orange slice. Serves 1.

SPARK PLUG

1 teaspoon Chartreuse liqueur
1 teaspoon brandy
1 teaspoon Calvados (see Note)
1 teaspoon apple liqueur
2 teaspoons verjuice
30 ml (1 fl oz) cloudy apple juice
juice of ½ lime
sliced green apple, for garnish

Place all the ingredients, except the sliced apple in a boston glass. Add 1 cup of ice cubes and shake for 10 seconds, then strain into a chilled martini glass. Garnish with the apple slices. Serves 1.

NOTE Cavaldos is an apple brandy from Normandy in France.

GRAPE MARTINI

10 white seedless grapes
1 teaspoon sugar syrup (see page 25)
45 ml (1½ fl oz) unoaked grappa
3 teaspoons dry Sherry (preferably fino)
2 teaspoons lemon juice
2 red grapes, for garnish

Place the white grapes and sugar syrup in a boston glass
and muddle. Add the grappa, sherry and lemon juice. Add
1 cup of ice cubes and shake for 10 seconds. Double strain
into a chilled martini glass. Skewer the red grapes onto a
toothpick and garnish. Serves 1.

CROWN STREET COOLER

30 ml (1 fl oz) cachaça (see Note)
20 ml (⅔ fl oz) Pommeau de Normandie (see Note)
30 ml (1 fl oz) apple juice
juice of ½ lime
1 teaspoon sour apple liqueur
2 teaspoons soda water
lemongrass foam (see below), for garnish
finely grated lime zest, for garnish

Place the cachaça, Pommeau de Normandie, apple juice,
lime juice and sour apple liqueur in a boston glass. Shake
and strain into a tall glass filled with crushed ice. Top
with the soda water. Garnish with the lemongrass foam
and scatter over the lime zest. Serves 1.

NOTE Cachaça is a Brazilian spirit made from fermented
sugarcane. Pommeau de Normandie is a French apéritif of
unfermented cider mixed with Calvados.

LEMONGRASS FOAM

100 g (3½ oz) caster (superfine) sugar
3 stalks lemongrass
1 sheet gelatine, titanium strength

Soak the gelatine in cold water for 5 minutes or until
softened.

Place the sugar, lemongrass and 400 ml (14 fl oz) water
in a saucepan over medium heat. Cook until the sugar
is dissolved, then reduce the heat to low and cook for
15 minutes to infuse. Squeeze out the excess water from
the gelatine and add the gelatine to the pan, stirring until
dissolved. Strain and allow to cool.

Pour into a cream canister and charge twice. Set aside
until ready to serve. This recipe makes more than you
will need.

WATERSHIP UP

30 ml (1 fl oz) carrot and caraway infused vodka
(see below)
3 teaspoons honey vodka (such as Medos)
1 teaspoon ginger liqueur
1 teaspoon pedro ximénez (see Note)
juice of 1 orange
juice of ¼ lemon
dehydrated carrot strips (see below), for garnish

Place all the ingredients, except the carrot strips, in a boston glass. Add 1 cup of ice cubes and shake for 10 seconds, then strain into a chilled martini glass. Garnish with the dehydrated carrot strips. Serves 1.

NOTE Pedro ximénez is a sweet, dark sherry from Spain.

CARROT AND CARAWAY INFUSED VODKA

1 x 700 ml (24 fl oz) bottle vodka
2 carrots
10 caraway seeds

Peel and dice the carrot. Add the carrot and caraway seeds to the bottle of vodka and allow to infuse for at least 2 weeks.

DEHYDRATED CARROT STRIPS

1 carrot
30 g (1 oz) maltodextrin

Place the maltodextrin and 200 ml (7 fl oz) water in a small saucepan and heat until the maltodextrin is dissolved. Allow to cool.
    Peel the carrot and, using a mandolin, thinly slice lengthways. Dip the strips in the maltodextrin mixture, then place on a baking tray lined with baking paper. Dry in a dehydrator at 60°C (140°F) for 1 hour. Alternatively, place in the oven on the lowest temperature and leave until completely dry.

'GST' (GIN, SHERRY, TONIC)

30 ml (1 fl oz) tonic
30 ml (1 fl oz) fino sherry
20 ml (⅔ fl oz) gentiane liqueur (see Note)
3 teaspoons gin
1 teaspoon lemon juice
1 strip of orange peel, white pith removed,
for garnish

Place all the ingredients, except the orange peel, in a boston glass. Add 1 cup of ice cubes and stir until combined and chilled. Strain into an tumbler filled with ice cubes. Garnish with the orange peel. Serves 1.

NOTE Gentiane liqueur is made from the gentian plant and has a medicinal taste.

AMANDA OUT

4 coriander seeds
30 ml (1 fl oz) gin
20 ml (⅔ fl oz) verjuice
1 teaspoon brandy
1 teaspoon Amaro Montenegro (see Note)
1 teaspoon Grand Marnier
juice of 1 mandarin

Place the coriander seeds in a boston glass and muddle. Add the remaining ingredients. Add 1 cup of ice cubes and shake for 10 seconds. Double strain into a chilled martini glass. Serves 1.

NOTE Amaro Montenegro is a type of amaro from Bologna in Italy. Amaro is a digestif made from herbs.

JUNIPER SMASH

4 juniper berries
30 ml (1 fl oz) pink grapefruit juice
30 ml (1 fl oz) Zubrowka vodka (see Note)
3 teaspoons gin
1 teaspoon sloe gin (see Note)
1 teaspoon cherry liqueur
1 teaspoon lime juice
strip of pink grapefruit peel, white pith removed,
    for garnish

Place the juniper berries into a boston glass and muddle.
Add the remaining ingredients. Add 1 cup of ice cubes and
shake for 10 seconds. Double strain into a chilled martini
glass. Garnish with the grapefruit peel. Serves 1.

NOTE Zubrowka vodka is a Polish vodka infused with
bison grass. Sloe gin is infused with sloe berries, a type
of plum.

RHUBUBBLE

2 teaspoons rhubarb syrup (see below)
2 teaspoons lemon juice
2 teaspoons crème de cassis (blackcurrant liqueur)
sparkling white wine or Champagne, to top

Add the syrup, lemon juice and crème de cassis, one at a
time, to a tall glass, then top with sparkling white wine.
Serves 1.

RHUBARB SYRUP

1 stalk rhubarb, leaves trimmed
110 g (3¾ oz/½ cup) caster (superfine) sugar

Dice the rhubarb and place in a saucepan with the sugar
and 125 ml (4¼ fl oz/½ cup) of water. Bring to the boil,
then remove from the heat and allow to cool. Transfer the
mixture to an upright blender and blend until smooth.
Pass through a fine sieve. Store in an airtight container
for up to 3 days in the fridge. This recipe makes more
than you will need.

KLF (KAFFIR LIME FIZZ)

4 kaffir lime leaves, plus 1 extra for garnish
¼ Lebanese (short) cucmber, plus batons for garnish
40 ml (1¼ fl oz) gin
1 teaspoon fiano vermouth (see Note, page 237)
juice of ½ lime
2 teaspoons soda water

Place the lime leaves and cucumber in a boston glass and muddle. Add the gin, vermouth and lime juice. Add 1 cup of ice cubes and shake for 10 seconds. Pour into a tall glass filled with crushed ice and top with soda water. Garnish with the lime leaf and cucumber batons. Serves 1.

A L'ORANGE

juice of 1 lemon
30 ml (1 fl oz) vanilla-infused dark rum (see below)
1 teaspoon orange liqueur (such as Grand Marnier)
1 teaspoon apricot liqueur
1 teaspoon Licor 43 (see Note)
juice of 1 orange

Place the ingredients in a boston glass. Add 1 cup of ice cubes and shake for 10 seconds, then pour into a Champagne saucer. Serves 1.

NOTE Licor 43 is a sweet Spanish vanilla-flavoured after-dinner drink.

VANILLA-INFUSED DARK RUM

1 x 700 ml (24 fl oz) bottle dark rum
3 vanilla beans, split

Place the vanilla beans in the bottle of rum and leave to infuse for at least 3 days — the longer you leave it, the more intense the vanilla flavour will be.

FOOD AND WINE PAIRING

The philosophy at Bentley when matching wine to food is a simple one: use wines that will enhance the food and vice versa. Wine should season food and food should season wine. We look for wines that refresh the palate, as well as stimulate the senses. We look for handmade wines with personality.

To illustrate our philosophy, let's take one of our favourite food and wine pairings — the chestnut soup, foie gras, puffed wheat, pine nuts and pickled raisins (see page 111) matched to a bright fresh riesling — and look at why they work so well together. Below are the steps we go through to find the right match.

MATCH THE WINE TO THE PERSON

The first thing to keep in mind when choosing a wine to pair with food is that people want to drink wines that they are comfortable with. It's no use pushing a highly oxidative wine from the Jura on to a person who likes clean, fresh and dry semillons — they just won't like it.

PROCESS OF ELIMINATION

Our approach to food and wine pairing is essentially one of elimination. When a new dish is put on the menu, the dish is tasted with several different wines. Some wines work and others don't. Through this process the perfect match is usually found.

BALANCE THE ACIDITY AND SWEETNESS

The texture and richness of the soup requires a wine with a high level of acidity. There is natural sweetness from the chestnuts, so the accompanying wine must also have at least the same level of sweetness or the wine will be lost. For this reason, all bone-dry wines, including semillons and most chardonnays, can be eliminated.

BALANCE THE OILINESS

The foie gras has a fatty, oiliness which coats the palate and leaves a distinctive and long aftertaste, so the wine needs to refresh the palate, which means when you have had a mouthful of the dish followed by a glass of wine, a neutral flavour returns to your mouth. White wines have the ability to refresh the palate more easily than red wines. The tannin and use of oak in red wines may also compete with the flavour of the foie gras and alter the overall taste. This means that all red wines can be eliminated, too.

YOUNG OR VINTAGE?

A fresh, young wine is essential as we want power and fruit to come though. Older wines need to be paired with simple food without too many intense flavours or the nuances and attributes of the wine can be overshadowed.

THE RIGHT MATCH

A young riesling is the obvious choice, one with a touch of sweetness to match the chesnut soup, plus enough body and richness to hold up against the foie gras. We are also looking for a wine to not only cleanse the palate but also to add something to the dish, in a way, to season the soup.

Germany, the home of riesling, produces many styles and types. Ones from the Mosel tend to have high acidity and fresh fruit flavours. This fits half of the criteria, but it also needs a riesling with body and weight. A suitable choice would be a drier riesling from the Pfalz, ideally a 'trocken' or dry style, which has a touch of sweetness.

The right match enables the dish and wine to talk to one another: the riesling adds acidity to the dish which is rich and textured. The wine cleanses the palate and enhances the soup. The dish also highlights the primary flavours, especially the crisp green apple, of the wine.

SOME FOOD AND WINE PAIRINGS

Kingfish marinated in squid ink with perfumed fruits and coconut The perfumed fruit needs a wine that can stand up to it. Try a pinot gris or for a special occasion, a Condrieu — an exotic, powerful viognier from the Rhône valley. The viognier injects its own characteristics while enhancing the dish. (See recipe, page 82.)

Black sesame and pea fondant with goat's curd dressing and snow peas This is a difficult dish to match. The dish doesn't sound like it's sweet, but there are some flavours that push it that way. Riesling works, but the best match is a Spanish albariño, which has bold flavours balanced by high acidity to cut through the dish, plus some residual sugar to counter the sweetness. (See recipe, page 98.)

Jerusualem artichoke custard with new season garlic and soy and borlotti beans A good dish to match because it works beautifully with many wines. My favourite match is a chenin blanc from the Loire Valley, in particular from Savennières. The high acidity of the grape cuts through the custard while the custard enhances the apple and pear fruit characters of the wine. (See recipe, page 103.)

Almond gazpacho with milk crisp and oyster The soup contains sherry vinegar which is an enemy of many wines. The sweetness and acidity of a German riesling handles this well, cleanses the palate and provides a background note to the flavours of the dish. (See recipe, page 88.)

Slow-cooked pork belly with apple, tonka bean and red miso The fattiness of the pork, plus the apple and olive flavours, make this a difficult dish to match. There are two very different options: red Burgundy with a bit of guts, such as those from Nuits-Saint-Georges, or an artisan cider. The red hugs the flavour of the dish, whereas the cider introduces a background note. (See recipe, page 104.)

Roasted spatchcock with sweetcorn polenta, pistachio and asparagus This works beautifully with a cool-climate shiraz, especially from the new-wave of small producers from Victoria. The dish needs a wine with a bit of grunt (but not so much that it will overpower some of the dish's more subtle flavours) and one with spice to highlight the sweet spatchcock. (See recipe, page 130.)

Roasted black angus sirloin with smoked leek, black fungi and kohlrabi purée This needs a wine which will walk hand in hand with the dish to the finish. It needs a wine with similar earthy undertones as the dish and it must also have enough fruit to overcome the natural sweetness of the leeks. A red from the southern Rhône is ideal but skip those with brooding alcohol and oak, go for a natural style instead. (See recipe, page 164.)

Toast custard with chocolate parfait and lychee purée The obvious choice is a fortified red: Banyuls, Rutherglen muscat, pedro ximénez and Port all work well, but matching chocolate to a fortified can be a bit of a cliché. The spirit Chartreuse V.E.P. is my choice as it can stand up to the rich, full chocolate and caramel flavours and adds a layer of complexity to the dish. (See recipe, page 190.)

Carrot cake with black olive sorbet All of the components are fairly easy to match with the exception of the black olive sorbet. Madeira is the most suitable choice, in particular a special-reserve verdehlo. This blankets the flavours without killing them while refreshing the palate at the same time. (See recipe, page 206.)

Poached peach with blueberries and magnolia ice cream There are plenty of both intense and subtle flavors in this dish. It needs a wine with power yet elegance. A Hungarian Tokaji works well, as it has the power and richness to cope with the fuller flavours, yet enough acidity to refresh the palate. (See recipe, page 214.)

ACKNOWLEDGEMENTS

This book is dedicated to our families. The time and many sacrifices it takes to run a restaurant like ours cannot be described and our families have been by our side every step of the way.

To my wife Fleur and my family Gary, Rosalie, Krysten and Ainsley. Brent

To my wife Anna, my kids Jaime and Maxim and my family Bruce, Lesley and Brett. Nick

When Nick and I decided to open the restaurant in 2006, there were two vital people who helped make our dream become a reality. Without the faith of our business partners **Bruce Hildebrandt** and **Geoff Squires**, their trust in our vision and their time and support, we would not have been able to create Bentley.

From the beginning, I knew this book would be a challenge. I have never written a book before, so I had to learn fast. None of my recipes had ever been documented, so I had to find a way to write and test 100 recipes on top of the day-to-day running of the restaurant. There was only one way this was going to be achieved, and it's the way the restaurant has always thrived, which is through the dedication and team work of the staff. I have always been very fortunate to have exceptionally committed and experienced staff who are willing to go the extra distance whenever called upon.

To my kitchen staff, who have been amazing through this process, frequently giving up their weekends, and who have, on occasion, worked up to a month without a day off. I don't know if I've ever worked with such devoted people. Your efforts are always appreciated and never unnoticed. At the head of the kitchen team is sous chef **Tim Bartholomew**. Not only has he been the longest standing staff member, but he has always led the brigade by example with his loyalty, talent and patience. Thanks goes to **Matt Fitzgerald** who returned to Bentley just in time for the shooting of this book, and **Aiden Stevens**, who does a fantastic job working with me on desserts, despite not having a formal pastry background, as it's one of the more difficult sections of our kitchen. My gratitude also goes to **Amir Jamil** and **Liam O'Brien** who offered support in the kitchen wherever it was needed. I have never underestimated the worth of my team.

Of course no restaurant can be successful without the floor and kitchen working together as one. My thanks and respect goes to the knowledgeable and accomplished service staff. No food is ever done justice without professional delivery. Fortunately, I feel confident every time a plate is sent from the kitchen to a customer, because I know the passionate, front-of-house staff deliver it with panache and style. Thank you to manager **Glen Goodwin** and his support team **Abby Goodwin**, **Kylie Javier** and **James Snelgrove**. A special thanks to **Kylie** for transcribing my thoughts and words into what you read in this book.

In addition to the current kitchen and floor teams, there have been many people who have contributed to making Bentley into what it is today. Previous staff members **David Myers**, **Dave Verheul** and **Dan Hong** have played an integral part, along with **David Wasserman**, who has been with Bentley from the beginning and is continually committed to our business.

There are many friends of the restaurant, including **Andrew Guard**, **Tim Stock**, **David Burkitt**, **Derek Nicholson**, **John Velutti**, **Anita Puharich**, **Igor Ivanovic**, **Pascale Gomes-McNabb** and **Ned Goodwin** who have all been incredibly supportive.

Ultimately the people that make Bentley what it is are our customers. They guide what we do and are our biggest supporters and toughest critics. Our regulars are the best in town.

However well you write a recipe, the story is told in the pictures of the book. When the book came about, I was able to pick my own photographer, **Luke Burgess**, who has been an integral part of this project. Having worked together in the past, there was a trust and respect for each other's work. His understanding of my style and ethos meant he was able to capture the essence of each dish and bring it to life.

And finally, to all the staff at Murdoch Books who have made this book possible, especially **Hugh Ford**, **Belinda So**, **Jane Lawson**, **Kay Scarlett**, **David Morgan** and, of course, **Juliet Rogers**.

INDEX

á l'orange 245
abalone, baby 117
acetate
    chocolate tubes 201
    foie gras parfait 111
    rhubarb custard 216
    yoghurt cream 194
agar agar 26
    beetroot gel 124, 176
    carrot purée 209
    coconut purée 82
    coffee purée 224
    dried fruit paste 90
    emulsified red miso oil 107
    lychee purée 190
    mandarin purée 81
    potato and almond nougat 173
    sour orange sauce 140
    strawberry purée 199
aïoli 24
almond bread crunch 65
almond gazpacho with milk crisp
    and oyster 89, 248
almond sauce 150
Amanda out 241
apple and green olive salsa 107
apple salad 38
apple and tonka bean jelly 104
artichokes
    baby globe artichoke and
        samphire 156
    hapuka with baby globe artichoke
        and squid ink crumbs 155–6
    Jerusalem artichoke custard 103
    slow-cooked Berkshire pork neck
        with pine mushrooms and
        purple congo potato purée 149
asparagus, truffled 57
avocado purée 44

baby globe artichokes and
    samphire 156
bacalao, poached, with smoked potato
    mousse and pipis 123
banana milk 185
barberry sauce 119

basil pudding with sweetcorn and
    zucchini flower salad 94–7
basil water 94
bass groper with sour orange,
    mussels, clams and mustard
    purée 139–40
beef
    braised wagyu beef cheek with
        burnt onion 'mayonnaise'
        and kale 159
    roasted black angus sirloin with
        smoked leek, black fungi and
        kohlrabi purée 165–6, 248
beetroot, smoked 168
beetroot gel 124, 176
beetroot purée 168
beetroot and salmon 'ravioli' 127
Berkshire pork neck, slow-cooked,
    with pine mushrooms and purple
    congo potato purée 149
beurre noisette 224
black angus sirloin, roasted, with
    smoked leek, black fungi and
    kohlrabi purée 165–6, 248
black bean dressing 34
black olive purée 155
black olive sorbet 206–9
black pastry crumbs 215
black sesame glass 98
black sesame and pea fondant
    with goat's curd and snow peas
    248, 98–9
black sesame purée 98
black truffles 174
blue swimmer crab and mango
    with black bean dressing 34
blueberry gel 215
bonito, pickled, with preserved lemon
    and apple 38
boudin noir with yabbies, mandarin
    and almond 81
burnt honey cream 189
burnt onion 'mayonnaise' 159

calamari with squid ink rice and
    green chilli salsa 37

calcium chloride 26
    chocolate spheres 212
    sweet liquid wasabi 61
    white bean and jamón 'gnocchi' 117
capers, dehydrated 20
caramelised pork cheek with beetroot
    and salmon 'ravioli' 124–7
carrot cake with black olive
    sorbet 206–9, 248
carrot and caraway infused
    vodka 241
carrot purée 209
carrot strips, dehydrated 241
cauliflower purée 86
celeriac, mushroom and almond
    'cannelloni' with saffron
    eschalots 150–2
celery jelly 49
celery salt 25
cheesecake with beurre noisette,
    coffee purée, cumquat and
    lemon meringue 223–4
cherry gel 228
cherry sorbet 229
chestnut cake 212
chestnut soup, foie gras, puffed
    wheat, pine nuts and pickled
    raisins 111–12
chicken
    chicken jus 22
    crisp spiced chicken with aïoli 72
    poached chicken with saffron
        eschalots, herb emulsion
        and jamòn crumbs 160–3
chickpea chips with garlic custard 69
chilli, green chilli and herb salsa 37
chocolate, honeycomb, bar 205
chocolate–cherry crumbs 231
chocolate cone with warm
    banana milk 185
chocolate ganache with orange oil,
    spice and salt 220
chocolate gel 200
chocolate ice cream 185
chocolate mousse 211
chocolate parfait 191
chocolate powder, frozen 211

chocolate spheres 212
chocolate tubes 201
chorizo and potato 75
cinnamon sugar 199
cocoa crumbs 191
coconut mousse with cherry sorbet
    and chocolate crumbs 228–31
coconut purée 82
cod and potato crostini 47
coffee and pistachio crumbs 206
coffee purée 224
confit garlic 24
crab, blue swimmer, and mango
    with black bean dressing 34
croûtons 44
Crown Street cooler 238

dai dai 60
daikon, pickled 60
dehydrating 20
dill oil 139
dried fruit paste 90
drinks
    á l'orange 245
    Amanda out 241
    carrot and caraway infused
        vodka 241
    Crown Street cooler 238
    frozen 'popcorn' Hemingway 234
    grape martini 238
    GST 241
    juniper smash 242
    KLF 245
    Mr Pink 237
    rhububble 242
    spark plug 237
    watership up 241
duck, roasted, with mushroom,
    cuttlefish and kombu gel 144–5

egg, soft free-range, with almond
    bread crunch and sherry caramel 65

feta balls 119
fish stock 23
foie gras parfait 111
food and wine pairing 247–8
frozen 'popcorn' Hemingway 234
fruit, perfumed 82

garlic
    confit garlic 24
    crisp garlic 76
    garlic custard 69
    new season garlic emulsion 123
    new season garlic with soy
        and borlotti beans 103
    roasted garlic purée 24
gazpacho three ways 30
gelatine 26
    blueberry gel 215
    burnt honey cream 189
    celery jelly 49
    cheesecake 224
    cherry gel 228
    chocolate mousse 211
    chocolate parfait 191
    coconut mousse 228
    emulsified red miso oil 107
    feta balls 119
    frozen 'popcorn' Hemingway 234
    honey jelly 186
    kombu gel 144
    lemongrass foam 238
    malted milk marshmallows 227
    orange blossom gel 206
    passionfruit marshmallows 227
    pea gel 99
    red pepper jelly 85
    rhubarb custard 216
    smoked eel parfait 48
    strawberry marshmallows 227
    toast custard 190
    Turkish delight 217
    yoghurt 85
    yoghurt cream 194
gellan gum 26
    Jerusalem artichoke custard 103
goat's curd dressing 97
grape martini 238
green gazpacho 30
green olive purée 107
GST 241
guar gum 26
    chocolate gel 200
    magnolia ice cream 215
    pineapple gel 201

hapuka with baby globe artichoke
    and squid ink crumbs 155–6
harissa 75
harissa spice mix 75

hazelnut purée 180
herbs
    herb emulsion 156, 163
    soft herb salad 108
honey jelly 186
honeycomb chocolate bar 205
horseradish purée 171
hot smoking 19

iota 26
    apple and tonka bean jelly 104
    celery jelly 49
    chocolate gel 200
    pineapple gel 201
isomalt 26
    black sesame glass 98
    lychee glass 190
    rhubarb tuiles 217

jamón crumbs 135, 160
jamón stock 114
Jerusalem artichoke custard with
    soy and borlotti beans 103, 248
juniper smash 242

kappa 26
    apple and tonka bean jelly 104
    chocolate gel 200
    smoked eel parfait 48
kingfish ceviche with pickled
    daikon and yuzu mayonnaise 60
kingfish marinated in squid ink
    with perfumed fruit and
    coconut 82, 248
KLF 245
kohlrabi purée 166
kombu 48, 49
    kombu chips 48
    kombu gel 144

lamb, slow-cooked rump, with
    kipfler potato and hazelnut 180
lamb stock 23
lecithin 26
    banana milk 185
lemon
    lemon meringue 223
    preserved lemon purée 38
lemongrass foam 238
licorice crumbs 200
licorice gel 200

liquid glucose 26
    black olive sorbet 206
    cherry sorbet 231
    chocolate parfait 191
    honeycomb 205
    magnolia ice cream 215
    pineapple sorbet 200
    rhubarb tuiles 217
    Turkish delight 217
liquid nitrogen 27
    frozen 'popcorn' Hemingway 234
liquid puff pastry 189
lotus root crisps 66
lychee glass 190
lychee purée 190

mackerel, citrus-glazed, with tartine
    of almond and soft herb salad 108
magnolia ice cream 215
malted milk marshmallows 227
maltodextrin 26
    black sesame glass 98
    celery salt 25
    dehydrated carrot strips 241
    lychee glass 190
    mandarin powder 197
    pea crumbs 98
Mandagery Creek venison, roasted,
    with spiced beetroot purée and
    mushrooms 168
mandarin ice cream 194
mandarin oil 197
mandarin powder 197
mandarin purée 81
marshmallows 227
methylcellulose 26
    basil pudding 94
    black sesame purée 98
    feta balls 119
    potato and almond nougat 173
    rose foam 217
    yoghurt 85
milk crisp 89
mint oil 99
miso rice balls 107
Mr Pink 237
mushrooms
    dehydrated 171
    pine mushroom, salsify and
      baby leek 174
mussels and clams with saffron
    sofrito 66

mustard cream 47
mustard dressing 103
mustard purée 139

olives
    apple and green olive salsa 107
    black olive purée 155
    black olive sorbet 206–9
    dehydrated black 139, 173
    green olive purée 107
    marinated 33
olive, sesame and chive crust 139
onions, burnt onion 'mayonnaise' 159
orange blossom gel 206
orange oil 65, 220
orange tapioca 90

Pacojet 27
    black olive sorbet 206
    cherry sorbet 231
parmesan crumbs 180
parmesan custard with truffled
    asparagus 57
passionfruit marshmallows 227
pastry
    black pastry crumbs 215
    liquid puff pastry 189
pea crumbs 98–9
pea gel 99
pea purée 98
peach, poached, with blueberries and
    magnolia ice cream 215, 248
pears, saffron-poached, with burnt
    honey cream and liquid puff
    pastry 186–9
pigeon, roasted, with pistachio,
    orange tapioca and dried
    fruit paste 90–3
pimentos de Padrón with sherry
    vinegar and garlic 76
pine mushroom, salsify and
    baby leek 174
pineapple
    liquid pineapple with soft
      chocolate and pineapple
      sorbet 200–1
    pineapple gel 201
    pineapple sorbet 200
    pineapple soup 201
pistachio cake, yoghurt cream and
    mandarin ice cream 194–7
pistachio praline 216

pistachio purée 90, 133
pork
    caramelised pork cheek with
      beetroot and salmon 'ravioli' 124–7
    pork bubble 104
    slow-cooked Berkshire pork neck,
      pine mushrooms and purple
      congo potato purée 149
slow-cooked pork belly with apple,
    tonka bean and red miso 104, 248
slow-cooked pork tenderloin with
    quince purée, broccoli and
    prune sauce 136
potatoes
    crisp potato and chorizo 75
    potato–yoghurt purée 155
    smoked potato 135
    smoked potato mousse 123
    warm potato and almond nougat
      with black truffle sauce and
      pine mushroom 173–4
prawn on a stick with black and
    white sesame 52
prune sauce 136
puffed wheat 111
pumpkin ice cream 223
purple congo potato purée 149

quail, 'roasted', with silverbeet,
    quinoa, feta and barberry 119
quince purée 136

raisins, pickled 111
red gazpacho 30
red miso oil 104, 107
    emulsified 107
red mullet with white bean and jamón
    'gnocchi' and saffron 114–17
red pepper crumbs 85
red pepper jelly 85
red wine jus 24
red wine sauce 165
rhubarb 242
    rhubarb custard and tuile and
      vanilla bean ice cream 216–17
    rhubarb juice and purée 216
    rhubarb syrup 242
    rhubarb tuiles 217
ricotta dumplings, hot 199
rose foam 217

saffron eschalots 152, 163
saffron sauce 114
saffron sofrito 66
saffron-poached pears with burnt honey
    cream and liquid puff pastry 186–9
saffron poaching liquid 186
salads
    apple salad
    seaweed and mustard cress
        salad 49
    yabbie salad 81
salmon, king, roasted with white
    asparagus, roasted beetroot
    and turnip 176–9
seaweed and mustard cress salad 49
semolina crackers 57
sherry caramel 65
sherry vinaigrette 61
smoked eel parfait with white soy
    dressing and seaweed 48–9
snapper, baby, with sweetcorn,
    zucchini flower, black fungi
    and squid ink 143
sodium alginate 26
    chocolate spheres 212
    sweet liquid wasabi 61
    white bean and jamón
        'gnocchi' 117
sodium citrate 26
    sweet liquid wasabi 61
sour orange sauce 140
sous-vide cooking 16
spatchcock, roasted, with sweetcorn
    polenta, pistachio and
    asparagus 130–3, 248
spiced cauliflower 86
squid ink crumbs 155
squid ink dressing 44
squid ink rice 37
squid ink sauce 143
stabiliser 26
    chocolate ice cream 185
    tonka bean ice cream 211
    vanilla bean ice cream 216
stocks 246–7
strawberry marshmallows 227
strawberry purée 199
sugar syrup 25
sweetcorn polenta 130
sweetcorn purée 94, 143

Thermomix 27
    rhubarb custard 216
    rhubarb tuiles 217
toast custard with chocolate parfait
    and lychee purée 190–1, 248
togarashi pepper 60
tomato dressing 44
tomato powder, freeze-dried 41
tonka bean ice cream with
    chocolate and chestnut
    cake 211–12
tonka bean mayonnaise 135
trimoline 26
    black olive sorbet 206–9
    cherry sorbet 231
    chocolate ice cream 185
    magnolia ice cream 215
trout roe vinaigrette 127
truffled asparagus 57
tuna
    seared, with tonka bean
        mayonnaise, smoked potato
        and jamón crumbs 135
    tuna tartare with tomato and
        squid ink 44
    yellowfin tuna with red pepper
        crumbs, yoghurt and
        anchovy 85–6
Turkish delight 217

vanilla bean ice cream 216
veal jus 24
venison
roasted Mandagery Creek venison
    with spiced beetroot purée
    and mushrooms 168
venison tartare with sweet liquid
    wasabi 61
verjuice sauce 145

wagyu beef cheek, braised, with
    burnt onion 'mayonnaise
    and kale 159
wakame, dehydrated 114
walnut jus 149
watership up 241
white anchovy sticks
    with pistachio praline 41
    with tomato and paprika 41
white bean and jamón 'gnocchi' 117
white chicken stock 22
white gazpacho 30

white soy dressing 49
wine, to pair with food 23–4

xanthan gum 27
    almond gazpacho 89
    almond sauce 150
    apple and tonka bean jelly 104
    barberry sauce 119
    black sesame glass 98
    black sesame purée 98
    black truffle 174
    burnt onion 'mayonnaise' 159
    feta balls 119
    pineapple soup 201
    potato and almond nougat 173
    rhubarb tuiles 217
    rose foam 217
    smoked potato mousse 123
    sour orange sauce 140
    verjuice sauce 145
    white soy dressing 49
    yoghurt 85

yabbie salad 81
yabbies 81
yellowfin tuna with red pepper
    crumbs, yoghurt and
    anchovy 85–6
yoghurt cream 194
yuzu mayonnaise 60

Published in 2010 by Murdoch Books Pty Limited

Murdoch Books Australia
Pier 8/9, 23 Hickson Road
Millers Point NSW 2000
Phone: +61 (0) 2 8220 2000
Fax: +61 (0) 2 8220 2558
www.murdochbooks.com.au

Murdoch Books UK Limited
Erico House, 6th Floor
93–99 Upper Richmond Road
Putney, London SW15 2TG
Phone: +44 (0) 20 8785 5995
Fax: +44 (0) 20 8785 5985
www.murdochbooks.co.uk

Publishing Director: Kay Scarlett
Photographer: Luke Burgess
Concept and Design: Hugh Ford
Project Manager and Editor: Belinda So
Production: Kita George

National Library of Australia Cataloguing-in-Publication Data

Author:	Savage, Brent.
Title:	Bentley: Contemporary Cuisine.
ISBN:	978-1-74196-817-0 (hbk.)
Notes:	Includes index.
Subjects:	Cookery, Australian.
Other authors/contributors:	Hildebrandt, Nick.
Dewey Number:	641.5994

A catalogue record for this book is available from the British Library.

Printed by 1010 Printing International Limited, China.

Colour reproduction by Splitting Image, Vic.

IMPORTANT: Those who might be at risk from the effects of salmonella poisoning (the
elderly, pregnant women, young children and those suffering from immune deficiency
diseases) should consult their doctor with any concerns about eating raw eggs.

OVEN GUIDE: You may find cooking times vary depending on the oven you are using.
For fan-forced ovens, as a general rule, set the oven temperature to 20°C (35°F) lower than
indicated in the recipe.

The Publisher and author would like to thank Hale Imports and Steelite International for
lending equipment for use for photography.